A HUMANE SOCIETY

A Humane Society

Edited by

STUART E. ROSENBERG

PUBLISHED FOR BETH TZEDEC CONGREGATION

BY UNIVERSITY OF TORONTO PRESS

Copyright, Canada, 1962, by
University of Toronto Press
Printed in Canada
Reprinted in 2018
ISBN 978-1-4875-7331-7 (paper)

Dedicated to

PHILIP *and* RACHEL FIRESTONE

By their children,
Whose generosity has made possible
the publication of this volume

Editorial Note

This volume contains essays based on the series of lectures delivered at the First Annual Institute of Ethics and the Sixth Annual Institute of Religion conducted by Beth Tzedec Congregation, Toronto, Canada, during 1961.

Each chapter in this volume represents solely the individual opinion of the author. The Institute, the Congregation, the editor, and the publishers do not assume responsibility for the views expressed.

We have been fortunate to enlist a group of authors, each of whom has distinctive knowledge in his own field. The Institute of Beth Tzedec Congregation is indeed grateful for the generous way in which they have responded to its invitation.

Foreword

by LOUIS FINKELSTEIN
Chancellor, Jewish Theological Seminary of America

Like the Institute of Ethics at the Jewish Theological Seminary of America after which it has been modeled, the Beth Tzedec Institute of Ethics, arranged by Dr. Stuart Rosenberg, has for its purpose the exploration of one of the most perplexing problems of our time—the application of traditional ethical insights to the actual problems of today. It is strange indeed, that in an age when, granted such insights, man may achieve an unprecedented degree of happiness and prosperity, and, lacking them, may court disaster for the present and future generations, ethics is one of the most neglected academic subjects. Almost nowhere in the modern world is any effective attempt being made to discover the answer to the question, raised by the ancient Rabbinic Sage, "What is the way which man ought to choose for himself?"

Perhaps this problem is being neglected because it cannot be approached except through new methods, unknown in previous ages. The modern academic theoretician is by virtue of his profession further removed from the process of daily decision-making than most men; and the modern decision-maker is further removed from access to theoretical discussion than almost any of his predecessors in civilized times and countries. Plato's ideal of the philosopher-kings might have led to the emergence of people who were mediocre in the skills both of government and of thought. But surely complete separation of philosophy (in its original sense of the love for wisdom) from great decisions leaves the practitioners of the former in a condition of futility, and those of the latter without access to man's profoundest thought on the goals he should pursue.

One possibility of meeting the problem of the separation of the theory of ethics from the problems of practical life has been suggested in the assembling of scholars and leaders in human affairs to discuss problems of daily life. Out of such assemblages of scholars in different fields with practical men with diverse concerns, there might emerge the type of wisdom needed to avert disaster in our time and for future generations.

The moralist, whose life has been spent in the study of the accumulated wisdom of the ages, need not retreat from his traditional calling into semantic speculation as to the precise meaning of the words "good" and "right." It is true that, in order to guide people, whatever his particular background, whether it be the study of a specific religious tradition or philosophy, the ethicist needs access to data, and methods of appraising data, which fall beyond his domain. It is also true that the master of such data and modern methods of scientific research can scarcely translate his knowledge into guides for peoples' lives and actions, until he has an appreciation of the goal he seeks to serve, which neither the data nor the methods of research can provide. It may almost be said that in our time the masters of religious and philosophical learning have much to communicate, but possess no means of communication, for their insights appear irrelevant to the urgent issues of the world. On the other hand, the scientist and technologist, whose discoveries answer such urgent questions, can communicate with the leaders and masses of men very easily, but lack the knowledge needed to communicate in the most important aspects of our individual and public lives.

It is the underlying premise of this book that the science of ethics, like that of jurisprudence, has to draw very largely on precedent for moral guidance. And yet, in drawing on moral precedent, ethics, once more like jurisprudence, must be free to apply the implications of what has been thought through, to novel and unprecedented situations. The effort to discover the means for utilizing precedent as a guide, without permitting it to become a ball and chain, is one which itself calls for the utmost wisdom we can muster. The jurists have solved this problem; in every civilized land, they are guided at once by the experience of the past, and at the same time feel free to interpret that experience in the light of new needs and new situations. The moralists, dealing with a broader spectrum of action, need to master this technique and to apply it to their domain.

While the role of the moralist in our time thus bears a resemblance to that of the jurist, it is far more complicated. The jurist, after all, has before him a situation where his authority and responsibility are limited. He has to apply justice in the case before him, on the basis of available data and available knowledge of precedent in his particular national tradition. If he errs, generally speaking, no great harm will occur; provided that his search for justice (as understood in his tradition) has been honest and sincere. The moralist's problem is to transform every man into a jurist, deciding for himself innumerable issues which appear before him each day; and on the decisions of which far more may depend than even the life of a particular individual.

Thus, our age is certainly not the first when races, long exposed to subjection and indignity, have demanded equality with those who formerly looked upon them as inferiors. The precedents and maxims formulated for approaching such problems abound in every philosophical and religious tradition. But ours is the first age when subject peoples, *all over the world*, are making the same demand at the same time.

The inevitable change which must come about in the relation of the Caucasian race to the pigmented ones involves basic moral problems, such as how to prevent those long subject to insult and indignity from using their hard-won recognition as a weapon, or from taking revenge on those who formerly oppressed them. Far outnumbering the former masters of the world, the newly developing peoples and races may, in their inexperience, be tempted not merely to seek equality, but to perpetuate injustice. Something like this has happened in lands which have undergone revolutions. The secret police of the Communist governments may be more efficient than that of the Tsars, but for a time at least their methods were not essentially different.

The task of the moralist of our time, in this area, is to help guide the liberation of the oppressed, and, at the same time, free them from the desire to become oppressors in their turn.

To achieve this difficult goal, the moralist needs access to all traditional wisdom, and to a great deal of modern knowledge, unavailable to the ancient or mediaeval, or even more modern ethical theorists.

To take another example, I do not suppose one American in ten thousand, when he considers the remarkable venom of the Chinese Communists to the United States, recalls that for decades the United States had on its statute books a Chinese Exclusion Act, forbidding any Chinese to enter its land. Had such an act been directed against any other people, their anger would doubtless have flared into vehemence long before the Chinese Communist revolution. As it is, it slumbered in the minds and hearts of that patient people, until a small group of revolutionary leaders chose to fan it into a flame, threatening to consume a large part of the world.

The moralist's task in this instance is even more formidable. The evil, out of which has now grown an overwhelmingly greater one, has been perpetrated, and cannot be recalled. Yet the potential enemy has to be transformed into a friend. This would be difficult even if only two individuals were involved. How is such a task to be accomplished between two nations, each most formidable, and each growing more formidable with every passing year?

Perhaps few citizens of the United States know that even now the country owes the Philippine Republic $73,000,000 in war damages. President after President has, since the War, urged payment of this debt. Congress has recognized its validity. But Congress has also consistently removed authorization to pay it from the annual budget of the country. The history of the relation of white to pigmented races being what it is, such a failure on our part may easily raise wonder in the minds of many citizens of the Philippines whether such treatment would also be meted out to a nation of Western Europe, which shares America's ethnic as well as cultural background.

The moralist's task in this instance may seem extremely easy; for the case of the Philippines seems just beyond question. Yet, the failure of the Congress of the United States to authorize payment of this debt year after year, despite the appeals of a succession of Presidents, cannot be without some reason, which requires exploration and evaluation.

The problems revolving about extending help to the needy have given concern to moralists in all generations, and in many traditions. It is almost inevitable that the one in a position to offer assistance should regard himself as in some way superior to the one dependent on him. Samuel Johnson had something to say about this to Lord Chesterfield, in a letter which has become world-famous. To help a brother who is in need, and at the same time to recognize whatever qualities in him give him a right to claim equality and even superiority, is by no means easy. But without mastering this skill, the aid which the United States is lavishing on lands which need it, turns to poison and wormwood. Such civilizations as that of India may be far poorer than that of the West in all material senses, but they are the equals of the West, if not its superiors, in some moral insights.

The study of traditional ethical systems would readily lead to the discovery of what is a suitable relation between donor and recipient of material aid. The study of the contemporary human situation would doubtless lead to the discovery of where the material aid could most effectively be employed.

The nature of the traditional moral systems, and their role in the world, and indeed, the discovery that they have a role, might profoundly affect not only international, but also private attitudes. In an era of rapid and accelerating change, of new discoveries and inventions, it is natural that one should wonder whether there is a corpus of traditional wisdom, even one which has constantly to grow. It is easy to think of ourselves as living in a new world, where the Moral Law no longer applies. Some of our biological and even cultural impulses encourage us to follow this conviction. Wisdom always seems to be getting in the way of what one really desires to do. Poor Dora in *David Copperfield* simply does not want to be wise, and prefers leaving both the burdens and the responsibilities of wisdom to her husband. It cannot be said that the modern world is as innocent of worldly wisdom as Dora, but a world which has witnessed two unprecedently destructive wars, and is vigorously preparing for a third, can scarcely suppose that it is really wise.

Yet the folly of modern nations is simply the sum-total of the national and international folly of the citizens of the world. We all know that peril lurks for the young at both ends of the social and economic spectrum. And if we had any doubt about this, we would merely have to study the history of great dynasties, all of which were founded by men of vigour and insight, and usually were destroyed by their descendants, who lacked even the moral strength required to sustain the enterprise of their fathers. It will be generally admitted that Mattathias and his sons were probably unusually gifted men. Alone, they managed to rouse the ardour of their tiny people, so as to compel the overwhelmingly larger and more powerful Syrian Empire to grant them freedom to practise their faith and ultimately, even a large degree of independence. But the great-grandchildren of Mattathias, such as Alexander Jannaeus, were scoundrels. And the great-great grandchildren were too weak even to hold the power bequeathed to them, and lost their kingdom to the Romans and Herod. What stood between the founders of the Hasmonean dynasty and the later weak generations was simply success. Extreme adversity might have had the same result.

All of us, knowing this, do our best to protect our descendants from impoverishment, but nothing to protect them from the similar perils of success. Each of us hopes that in some way the perils which lurk at the prosperous end of the economic spectrum will through some miracle leave our own progeny unhurt.

Yet giving one's all to the poor is not an answer to the dilemma of the man of wealth, who wishes to protect his descendants against moral and intellectual softness. The descendants, disinherited, may become bitter against their ancestor, and deliberately pursue purely hedonistic courses in life. The moral dilemma of wealth, however, has to be faced, like the moral dilemma of poverty. Some successful people in the past preserved their children and grandchildren from the perils bequeathed to them; as some poor people preserved their descendants from the spiritual decadence sometimes involved in poverty.

But to master the art of bequeathing material success, without bequeathing with it spiritual and moral failure, requires guidance, study, research, and dedication to a cause few of us recognize as such.

The reader of the various essays in the present volume will not find answers to moral problems of our time. But he will discover how thoughtful and good men are analysing them. This is not a manual, to take with one, so as to find one's way among the perplexities of our time. But it is a very good book to read again and again, to rouse oneself from complacency, to stimulate one's mind for concern with the greatest of the sciences, namely the Science of Life, and the greatest of all arts, namely, the Art of Life.

Contents

EDITORIAL NOTE — vii

FOREWORD. Louis Finkelstein — ix

PART ONE: THE PERSONAL LIFE

1 / A Humane Society. Stuart E. Rosenberg — 3

2 / Freedom of Choice: The Ethics of Personal Responsibility. Brock Chisholm — 13

3 / The Ethical Goals of Modern Education. Murray G. Ross — 28

PART TWO: GROUP RELATIONS

4 / The Moral Challenge of Underdeveloped Peoples. Mordecai W. Johnson — 49

5 / Legislating Human Rights in Ontario: I. Louis Fine — 66

6 / Legislating Human Rights in Ontario: II. Thomas M. Eberlee — 75

PART THREE: GOVERNMENT

7 / Communicating the Truth: Ethical Dilemmas of Radio and Television. ANDREW STEWART — 87

8 / Ethical Problems in Politics. PAUL H. DOUGLAS — 101

9 / Religious Ethics and Foreign Policy. JOHN C. BENNETT — 114

10 / The Ethical Necessity of Defending Democracy. PAUL H. DOUGLAS — 127

PART FOUR: THE JEWISH CONTRIBUTION

11 / Jews and the Nations of the World. BERNARD MANDELBAUM — 141

12 / Ethical Considerations in the Shaping of Jewish Life. SIMON GREENBERG — 152

CONTRIBUTORS — 165

Part One: The Personal Life

STUART E. ROSENBERG

BROCK CHISHOLM

MURRAY G. ROSS

1 / A Humane Society

STUART E. ROSENBERG

In establishing its First Annual Institute of Ethics, which provided the occasion for the initial preparation of these essays, Beth Tzedec Congregation took as its model similar programmes of the Institute of Religious and Social Studies of the Jewish Theological Seminary of America. The Congregation has opened its doors to all men and women of the community of which it is part, in an effort to serve the broadest and widest interests of the total Canadian community. We have, therefore, invited to our platform and to our study-circles men who have emerged from a variety of different experiences, to help illumine a number of problems perplexing us all. These lectures were stimulating when first heard and they are offered here in printed form in the hope that they may become part of the current literature of ethical concern.

The discussions which the Institute evoked may not have brought us to final conclusions. But they were undertaken in the first place without so naïve a hope. They have done something more necessary, more possible, even more important. They have helped sharpen the judgment that unless the current "religious revival" is converted into an ethical revival, religion can surely mean very little to anyone. Without an advance towards a more humane society, there can be no true return to God.

The simple truth stares us squarely in the face: despite the seeming success of organized religion, most people are still ethically and religiously illiterate. We mouth religious slogans which we have imbibed in our childhood; but we fail to act upon them because we do not really understand them, in adult fashion. Unfortunately, we have learned religion much as we have learned how to walk—after we absorbed the fundamentals, we stopped thinking consciously about them. As adults, we no more ponder carefully what we mean when we spout religious phrases, than we stop to consider the fluent movement of one foot after the other.

Some people imagine that religion can be used, like any other item of consumer goods. All you need to do is reach for it, take it off the shelf, stir and serve: "Instant salvation," they label it. But when we use religion, instead of allowing it to use us, we always end up abusing it.

Some "use" religion as a prop to shore up sagging nervous systems. They rely upon it for the security and strength they refuse to achieve on their own. They would like to see life as neat and easy, a sweet and simple affair. So, they reach for "the Man Upstairs," as they would say, reduce Him to their size, and carry Him in their vest pocket—on the left side, nearest the heart, of course!

Others turn to religion as a respectable means of hallowing their hates, not their loves. Because of unhappy temperament, some thrive only in vindictive isolation, fenced off from their neighbours. They need wide barriers and high walls to be happy because, inside, they are so unhappy. They flee from the world because they are afraid of it. They cannot abide its open societies, its changing patterns, or the possibility of being persuaded by its convincing opinions. This kind of religion is "useful" because it is safe—safe from the challenge of involvement in the lives and needs of others. But it can only be "used" by "us," never by "them," and so, it is really an abuse of religion.

Still others, the dependent and the emotionally immature, imagine that they can quickly don a cloak of piety, grab the horns of the altar, and easily acquire foolproof protection from anxiety and trouble. They are looking for short-cuts to circumvent the touchy and thorny issues of life. Unfortunately, from what they have heard about religion from some of its overeager "salesmen," it appeals to their cowardly feelings, not to their courage. But this misuse of religion only succeeds in making weak people weaker still.

One can hardly imagine a spiritual renaissance that does not seek to assert the moral relevance of religion in the habit and affairs of men, communities, cultures and nations. It is in this arena, particularly, that the "return" seems to founder; it hardly ever gets off the ground. Often, the "religious-minded" deny their churches and synagogues the moral right to speak out on issues which are patently moral and spiritual. They demand that "the things of Caesar and of God" be permanently separated, and that the religious society stand aloof, on the sidelines of life, to deal only with the "business of the church." This "non-interventionist" attitude prohibits the freely organized religious communities from giving the kind of leadership to society which we are not getting elsewhere.

Racial tensions, anti-minority attitudes, indifference to international problems of great spiritual moment are often fostered within churches and synagogues whose members want a socially respectable, more than an ethically enlightened, religion. Instead of being converted by a church to a moral world-view, too many succeed in converting the church and the synagogue to their own prejudices, by declaring the really vital human issues to be out-of-bounds for the religious community.

Religion, thus, often properly comes under attack by those who label themselves "intellectuals." No one can argue the need for rationality in human affairs; we avoid the light at our own peril. Intellectuality, unhappily, is a sadly missed element in our political and cultural life. And yet, knowledge by itself can do harm rather than good; this is especially apparent when we observe the manner in which many modern intellectuals "ply their trade." They have succeeded in fragmentizing the world even as they have been successful in splitting the atom. In our day, the pursuit of knowledge is often equated with intensive specialization in fractional fields of investigation. The intellectuals are indeed right when they speak of the need for rationality in human behaviour. They are wrong when they identify wisdom with facts, insight with information, humaneness with knowledge. Indeed, our generation suffers not so much from a lack of knowledge, but rather from the absence of a passion for its righteous use.

A parable for these intellectuals was recently recorded in the daily press. The newspaper story of the untimely, accidental death of one of the world's great men sent a shiver down readers' spines. It was a parable, not an obituary; what really mattered was not that he died, but how he died. The report described how Sir Raymund Hart, the man who developed Britain's radar defence system at the outbreak of World War II, and one of the great geniuses in the field of electronics, came to his end: he picked up the live end of a 240-volt electrical connection while barefoot. "It was the sort of mistake a chap who could not change a fuse would be likely to make," said his son. "And yet my father, a genius in electronics, made just such a mistake. Maybe he became overconfident about electricity."

Of course, Sir Raymund may have been daydreaming while intricately involved in pondering a serious scientific problem and in the pursuit of the complicated got struck down by the obvious. Most likely, however, he made a foolish error in judgment; even scientists are prone to fatal mistakes, errors of judgment in their own area of expertness, which even laymen would not think of committing.

Ours is an "expert" society so highly involved and so technical that most of us leave decisions and conclusions to those whom we think are more competent. We worship the specialist and deify the technician. But, truth to tell, while they often look like gods, they sometimes act like fools. They take the adulation of the public far too seriously, imagining themselves really to be what the less-informed public thinks they are.

There are no greater follies than those of the so-called wise man. When he errs—he errs large! He may be sure of his knowledge; he is, often, much less sure of himself. Sometimes his over-concentration and "expertness" serve to trip him up; he thought he knew everything, and he should have known better.

Hitler's professors were men of great scientific achievement who stood in the forefront of human intellectual attainment. But they were capable of being used and prostituted to destroy human life barbarously, in cheap, efficient and scientific ways. They were outstanding technicians, but as men, they were dupes and knaves. They made no small, insignificant errors; theirs were big, massive—expert!

We admire proficiency and mastery and in our technological age, those who know a lot about precious little, reach top status. In blind unsophistication, we snub broad, humane knowledge in favour of "specialized" information. Or what is worse: we disqualify the good man on the grounds that he is not the best man. The obverse is more likely: the "best" man is not always a good man.

There are those, in addition to the intellectuals, who also consider their view of human progress as an all-sufficient approach. These look to the law as the principal way by which man's ethical and social dilemmas may be resolved.

Law, like rationality, is a necessary and vital force for human betterment. It is a valuable weapon, for it can coerce our worst nature by whipping it into better shape. Legislation for human progress is a significant and indispensable tool of the humane society. Yet the law cannot become a substitute for human will, for it functions only negatively, only when it has been broken. The crucial problem in the moral life of man centres upon the positives, not the negatives; not only upon overt actions but upon covert intentions. Too often, law but enshrines the lowest of our common denominators and necessarily avoids dealing with the "imagination of our heart"— the truly crucial centre of our moral or immoral activities.

Once, so the tale goes, a plague raged among the animals. The lion, ruler of the animal world, determined to set up court to discover who among his subjects had sinned, and was thus responsible for bringing the dreaded pestilence upon them all. All of the animals were summoned to appear before his majestic and august presence to confess their wrong-doing. The tiger, the wolf, and the bear openly admitted that they had maimed, destroyed, and killed animals and humans, without a shred of mercy. Despite their voluntary admission they were exonerated from all blame by the judge. Said the lion: "You are held guiltless since you have only done what is expected of you." Finally, the lamb made her appearance at court. The lion maintained a persistent and penetrating line of questioning. At last, the lamb did recall that on one particular occasion, because she was very hungry, she had eaten the straw which stuck out of the shepherd's shoe. Without further evidence or investigation the lion pounced on these words, and hotly pronounced the sentence of guilt. Roared he: "For this grievous sin of the lamb, this terrible disaster has befallen us all. We condemn her to violent death—to be torn apart by the bear, the tiger, and the wolf!"

The animal kingdom may have its own problems and thus abide by its own peculiar rules, but this is no excuse for man to emulate the beast. Law is the armour of the weak; it constitutes their only humane defence in the presence of the mighty. But it, too, is not immune from the selfish, haughty manipulation of the powerful. When the strong use the law as if it were intended to "protect" them from the weak, they destroy its spirit, using it to abuse it. Often, law gives unethical majorities legal but immoral power. Inevitably, there is an ethical lag between law and the achievement of a more humane society.

For all these reasons, the world, for its humanity, depends upon its majorities more than upon its minorities; more upon the weak than on the strong. Power corrupts man, distorts his vision, deflects his moral sense. Instead of seeking to protect the unprotected, the powerful turn the tables on them, exploit their weakness, make a joke of their frailty. But ultimately history foils the mighty because it is hinged to the law of "measure for measure." The strong ones may grow from strength to strength only to trip over their own power lines. Athens survived but Sparta fell, just as the ant thrives still, long after the dinosaur has toppled into oblivion. The meek can survive to inherit while the mighty fall under their own weight.

The witness of conscience is found in the "have-nots"; the "haves" are often too busy getting bigger. And so those who have something to offer society need not pine after bigness: the tragedy lies not in being small or outnumbered but in desiring to become "as big as the biggest," "as powerful as the mighty."

Majorities, then, have more to gain, less to lose when they encourage the rights of creative minorities within their midst. They can hope to survive only if they listen to what the powerless are saying and support their right to say it. Minorities may depend upon the majority for their right to live. But a majority needs its minorities even more; it depends upon them for its moral health and its ability to survive creatively.

It is therefore my conviction that the fundamental basis for ethical achievement is rooted in a religious attitude towards life. Unless a man can view his neighbour as an equal in the sight of the One God, as a fallible, faltering, co-creature in need of mutual sympathy, understanding, and love, neither the purely rational nor the purely legal approach to human betterment can avail us.

Religions were the first to teach love. But few adults have gone beyond a juvenile understanding of its truest, deepest significance. Unless we get to the core of its meaning we shall all probably die loving the wrong things, in the wrong ways. To survive, we need an adult Declaration of Love—one that will educate our hearts as successfully as we have educated our minds.

For those who still care, here is a suggested preamble to such a Declaration:

1. We pledge our lives in true faith, to seek to love people for what they are, not to reject them for what they are not.

2. We stake our belief in earnest on the proposition that unless we seek to love others in ways that earn their love, we ourselves cannot be loved.

3. We affirm with the fullness of our being the truth that real love requires real concern. Indifference to truth and kindness deflects our intentions, makes them into pious but ineffective syllables of solicitude.

4. We shall be firm with ourselves in guarding against self-righteousness and self-justification. Instead of asking "what's in it for me," we shall ask: what can we do to help?

5. Above all, we shall be patient, conciliatory, eager to forgive, ready to admit our own guilt and error.

And even those who "love" the world—their neighbours or strangers—according to crisp scriptural imperative must learn to couple love with freedom. When do you love your neighbour, and how? When he thinks as you do, prays as you do, votes as you do, acts as you do? If so, your love is not love—it is hate for differences, inverted as love for similarity. The real test of our protestations of love comes when we let him who must be himself, be himself—and love him for what he is; not for what he is not.

It is adult religion we need; no primitive, childish faith will do. And it is the business of church and synagogue to educate us all in these lessons of applied love. Unless the institutions of religion put the ethical issues of our day at the top of their agenda, they will be guilty of unpardonable irrelevance, of answering questions nobody is asking.

They must play an important role as the conservers of the ennobling values of the past. But they cannot be conservers without also being critics of values. They must not become vassals of the state, perennially pleading "me too," fearful that their criticism of prevailing political judgments and economic habits brand them as treacherous and unpatriotic. They must play a catalytic social role. Firmly planted within society, they must yet retain their independence, and refuse to be dominated or exploited by seekers after power. They must never become the ally of nationalism for nationalism's sake—the true religionist understands well that "patriotism is not enough." They should be as critical of values that make the individual the measure of all things, as of a system that exalts the state for the benefit of its bureaucracy. Their task is to help create individuals whose concerns are social; to mould societies whose goals are humane. And to achieve these ends, religious statesmanship is required—not mere churchmanship.

The adoption of such a role by organized religion can lead it to become the moral proponent of the open mind. The contribution of the scientific method has not been its material results alone, but its steady insistence upon the need to hear new evidence, all the time. To function congenially in such an age, religion cannot permit this approach to go unheeded. It cannot rest its case uttering sacred eurekas. Its past discoveries are important, but new discoveries are called for. It must strive to become the interpreter of every noble striving, every precious human insight. And in the service of such ideas, it must risk the possibilities of unpopularity. A religious institution that is willing to keep alive the *search* for truth, even under penalty of remaining in the minority, earns for itself a vital place in the lives of men. In things of the spirit, it may make bold to proclaim, numbers alone do not count.

No claim for finality or ultimate wisdom need be made by religious institutions in order to justify their earnest stake in seeking to answer man's ethical questions. Indeed, as this book will, it is hoped, testify, before they can honestly arrive at final answers, religious groups must first be ready and willing to ask the right questions.

2 / Freedom of Choice: The Ethics of Personal Responsibility

BROCK CHISHOLM

Freedom of choice is something with which man has had little or no previous experience, and we therefore need to do some clear thinking about it. Clear thinking, however, is invariably painful, because for practically no one has it been developed as a habit.

Each of us has been expected to follow the ancient patterns into which he happens to have been born, whatever the patterns happen to be, and no matter how queer they seem. It has been almost impossible for most people to change basic attitudes that were imposed on them in childhood, because very early in life these become conscious values strong enough to awaken feelings of shame and guilt if abandoned. For a very long time, human beings have uncritically accepted the patterns followed by their parents. A small number of people have rebelled, sometimes quite violently, even destructively. Yet, generally speaking, throughout human history basic attitudes have been marked by considerable consistency, from generation to generation. Although this consistency may have had merit in the past and may still have, the radical change in conditions which we must meet in our day raises serious questions about the continuing validity of patterns that may have been relatively harmless in the past but could be fatal now.

The world of our ancestors did not vary greatly from one generation to another. The village blacksmith's son would live in the same community and most often follow his father's occupation. This was normal for most men; they tended to fit themselves into the condition of life in which they found themselves. Throughout history, the survival of the human race was marked by a competition to death between different groups. Competition was the normal pattern of behaviour—the method by which man protected himself and helped to ensure the continuity of his group. The size of the group has changed over a long period of time but the method of self-preservation has remained almost exactly the same. Earlier in human history, the survival-group was the family, which was an integrated unit. Wars and feuds took place between various family groups fighting one another for space, for fishing areas, for farm land, for women, for cattle, or for whatever else their members wanted. All this was regarded, in the early years of human social development, as the normal way of getting along. In this competitive process, groups did manage to survive but very large numbers of people were killed. The survival-units developed along autonomous and sovereign lines. The head of the family, the patriarch, made the rules; his whims were law. Whatever he wanted was deemed good; what he did not want was considered bad. As the group became larger, the survival-group developed into the clan, the tribe, the city-state, the principality, the kingdom, the nation, the empire; yet each of these groups was still competing with other groups for survival and each was claiming sovereignty.

But something has happened in the past fifteen years which has changed this whole picture, something which has, in fact, rendered the earlier method of survival obsolete and exceedingly dangerous. One of the marks of this change is the invention of a new military term, "overkill," which simply means the capacity to kill more people than there are. We now have the weapons to kill every person in the world, as well as all other forms of life, at least three times over. There are even some people, apparently, who are able to contemplate the possibility of killing everybody ten times over—the view, however, is hard to support on any logical or reasonable basis.

Such a possibility was totally unknown to our ancestors. Quite suddenly the survival-unit has become not the family, the tribe, the clan, the city-state, the principality, nor even the nation, but the human race itself. A situation has now arisen where no group can defend itself against deadly attack from outside. The old competitive survival to the death has now become synonymous with racial suicide.

We have had no education in coping with this situation, and so we are not equipped to deal with it. We have hardly yet begun to realize that we are the first generation capable of destroying the entire human race. No previous one has ever held a veto over the continuation of human evolution, as we do. Our earlier concerns related to the welfare of single groups, however defined—whether by race, by colour, by religious denomination, by ideology, by geographical boundaries, or by some other standard involving much less than the entire race.

Thus when suddenly it becomes necessary for us to think in ways for which we receive no guidance from tradition, we find the process very confusing and difficult indeed. We have no conscious values to guide us with respect to this survival of the human race. We have no traditions and no institutions designed for this purpose, except the United Nations and its specialized agencies, which are but recent innovations. All of our other institutions were developed in a world quite different from this one, and for purposes that cannot any longer be effective. We have suddenly become members of the human race itself but our thinking and our feeling are as yet unable to comprehend this fact.

It was near the end of World War II when it began to be apparent to thinking people in many parts of the world that the human race had become extremely dangerous to itself. We come from people who have fought each other in every generation throughout all of human history; indeed, as we have seen, this has been one of the most consistent of our patterns of behaviour. For this "normal" and often "admirable" behaviour suddenly to become potentially so very dangerous has been deeply disturbing to many people; hence, most of the people in the world are loath to admit or look at it, or let themselves think about it. Of course, one recognizes this avoidance-mechanism as a sign of immaturity. It is not and cannot be effective, although many people have tried and still try to deal with threatening matters by using the so-called "ostrich" technique of hiding their head in the sand. (This, by the way, is a slander on the ostrich, which does not hide its head in the sand. It is a very sensible bird, and it would not have survived by such conduct!) Indeed, this remains one of the popular human methods for avoiding responsibility, decision, and thought about painful things.

The people of the world have had, of course, an effective training in not thinking about painful things. In North American cultures we can find several clear symbols of this, to which many children are exposed. One is the symbol of the three little monkeys sitting in a row, one with its hands over its ears, the second with its hand over its eyes, and the third with its hands over its mouth. We all know the accompanying text: "Hear no evil, see no evil, speak no evil." It is this attitude that has been one of the most disastrous held by man. This timidity, for example, kept syphilis alive as a great scourge to humanity for many years long after it could have been controlled—nobody wanted to talk, or hear about it. It was shut out of people's minds because the social unpleasantness kept ears and eyes closed to a medical need. But wherever there is evil, it is vastly important that it *should* be known, seen, and talked about, for only then can the decisions be made which will cope with it.

We are still very reluctant to take this kind of responsibility, and particularly in our new situation. It may be that man will not be able to accept his present responsibility, hitherto so unfamiliar to him. It may be that man is now in about the same position as some of the great animals like *Brontosaurus* shortly before they disappeared. Many forms of life have existed on earth for far longer than man and once flourished mightily. But many of them have disappeared and are known only by their fossil remains. In every such case it appears that the cause was the same: that particular form of life was not able to make an adequate adjustment to changed circumstances, or to take charge of the circumstances for its own benefit. Man has not yet proven his ability to survive under these new circumstances, for which he has not yet developed new instruments. Under these circumstances, the responsibility for great human problems cannot be turned over to the United Nations, or its specialized agencies, or to governments. The problems go too deeply into human nature and individual personality. The solutions must be achieved by large numbers of *individuals*—individuals who will have attained a level of maturity not required of any previous human generation.

At the end of World War II, the nations were frightened. It had quite suddenly been shown that we could destroy ourselves and, under the influence of that valid anxiety, the nations came together. They set up the United Nations and its specialized agencies in an attempt to experiment hopefully with new ways of living together and to learn how to live in peace. We have not yet proven that we can make the United Nations work effectively. The people at home have not yet changed enough to support the United Nations adequately in the jobs that need to be done. In meetings of the United Nations, of its committees, commissions, and specialized agencies, it has become common to hear delegates from many countries, including our own, make statements of which they are privately ashamed, statements given in order to gain prestige for their own governments or to acquire some unilateral economic, political, or military advantage. This is, frankly, a prostitution of the United Nations, which was not designed for such propaganda purposes. When any nation or group of nations so uses the United Nations, the United Nations does not work well. It was created to help people learn how to live together co-operatively for the general benefit, and not to help one group to gain an advantage over another.

When chief delegates who have been active for some years in international affairs and have come to know and respect people from other parts of the world, are required to make statements dictated by their foreign offices or state departments, statements not calculated to help the people of the world, but only their own people, their feeling of shame is inevitable. Many delegates even apologize in advance to their fellows from other parts of the world, whose opinion they value, for statements they are going to have to make. Delegates from Communist nations do this, as well as delegates from other countries. These delegates would seem to be becoming much more mature than their state departments or foreign offices or their people at home. I, indeed, know a number of delegates who have been withdrawn by their governments from the United Nations and its specialized agencies, apparently because they have become too civilized; they have begun to function as though they were not nationals, but members of the human race! Most governments in the world, and most people behind those governments, are, then, not yet ready to have their delegates act in mature and civilized ways. The implications of this observation are important: we cannot expect better work from the United Nations while the governments which comprise it are not willing to go any further than they are going now and, in many cases, are holding back their delegates. Whatever needs to be done in terms of international inter-human relationships must, therefore, be initiated by the people at home—inside our countries, in homes and schools and churches, wherever people come together.

The responsibility is ultimately individual, and in order to assume even a small part of it, the people of the world must achieve a level of individual maturity not envisaged until recently. This necessity has been set out in the Charter of the United Nations and in the constitutions of some of the specialized agencies. It is, for example, very clearly stated in the Constitution of the World Health Organization which, by the way, has been signed and ratified by about one hundred governments on behalf of practically all the people in the world. The first statement in that constitution is a definition of the word "health" (it is a definition which can even be taught to children with some confidence that it need not be changed—it now requires a two-thirds vote of the nations of the world to change the meaning of the word "health").

Health, then, is a state of complete physical, mental, and social well-being and not merely the absence of disease or infirmity. This is a new idea! To our ancestors, health was just not being sick—there were no positive requirements. This new definition indicates that the people of the world now expect from themselves a level of development, a degree of maturity not required at any previous time in human history. A little later in that same constitution there is another relevant statement, which says that the healthy development of the child is of basic importance—of course, again meaning physically, mentally, and socially, healthy. And then it goes on: "The ability to live harmoniously in a changing total environment is essential to such development." That is a very big order! Our ancestors have not been able to live harmoniously in any environment, even one that was not changing as rapidly as ours, nor have they been able to live at peace. It is interesting to note that these definitions were made by middle-aged or elderly people, who did not say that *they* proposed to learn how to live harmoniously in a changing total environment but placed that load of responsibility on children. Yet, it appears that this necessity is basic. Unless enough children now growing up can attain that exalted level of maturity, the probability of the survival of the human race in future generations is indeed very slight.

We come back to the disturbing fact that we cannot, with any confidence, go back to our ancestral behaviour patterns to find rules for this new living—our ancestors had no idea of this challenge and made no preparations for living effectively in this kind of world. Thus though we know that one of the most consistent patterns of human behaviour—warfare—(which has set up most of our great heroes)—has suddenly become suicidal, we have nothing as yet to substitute in its place. We have not evolved other methods of getting our own way, which is basically the function of warfare, is it not? Men have always had recourse to war when they could not get their own way by any other method. Now, however, we must reassess our assets and liabilities and so begin to understand ourselves better than we ever have before. We cannot afford merely to accept, without question, any or all of the attitudes of our ancestors, since we know that because of many of these same attitudes, in the past, warfare occurred. We cannot know which of the attitudes of the society into which we were born may still be useful or which have suddenly become very dangerous, unless we hold ourselves free to re-examine and re-think all of them.

This is not to say that it would be sensible to throw out all the wisdom of the past and discard it completely. To do so would be just as stupid as to accept all of its attitudes without question. The necessity is for us, on our own responsibility to decide for ourselves what of ancestral wisdom is still valid for our new situation, and what needs to be revised or given up. This means that we have to start questioning our own consciences, even the basic building blocks in our personalities. We may find that some of those particular building blocks, far in the depths of our personality, are not effective now but constitute a weakness because they prevent us from taking sensible action in the world of today. In the past, when situations did not change very much from one generation to another, men could afford to depend on their consciences to a considerable extent. Indeed, many people have been taught in their infancy and childhood that conscience is "a still small voice" that always speaks the truth—it is, according to this teaching, completely reliable. As with so many other things that we have been taught, this doctrine, too, needs to be looked at clearly. It is quite demonstrable that many consciences are not reliable at all in new situations because most people have not gone to the trouble of helping their conscience to become more mature; for them, "conscience" is simply what they believed when they were six or seven years old.

The content of our conscience is for each of us accidental—following the accident of the time, place, and family of our birth. No one has ever found a Presbyterian conscience in an Eskimo. If we had been born into another family, in a different place, or in a different town, on the other side of the mountain, the ocean or the railway tracks, we would have an entirely different set of certainties: just as sure, just as absolute—and just as accidental. Quite suddenly it has become necessary for mankind to decide—and to decide consciously and firmly—that we cannot continue to be the creatures of accident; it is too dangerous and is now almost certainly suicidal for the whole race. We can no longer depend on the ways in which we found security in the past. When we have become frightened we have always increased our armament, have always tried to get better clubs, bows, arrows, or spears; and now, more soldiers, bigger guns, or bigger atomic bombs. But to be able to kill more people is no answer any longer.

Once we kill everybody—including ourselves—it does not matter that we can kill more. The system of thought which depends on the ability to kill people with whom we have difficulty living has broken down; it is simply not available any longer, except at the expense of our own lives as well.

Here, then, is a very real problem for anyone who tries to think clearly about world problems today. We need to break through the prejudices that are supplied by every culture, sub-culture, and family, and which, generally speaking, we do not question because they have been made so absolute in our childhood. In order to break this pattern in ourselves, it becomes necessary actually to practise thinking—to practise thinking independently of the accident of one's birth; and this is not an easy thing to do. It can be done—a great many people have learned how to do it—but it is painful and difficult. This is not to suggest that we need give up local loyalties to our own people or group; it does suggest that we are going to have to take as a goal wider loyalties: loyalties which will encompass the human race itself, now our own responsibility.

As far as our consciences will allow us at present we do have freedom of choice here. Too often, however, our consciences get in the way. Unfortunately, we misuse words; to call a person an "internationalist" in many parts of the world is to suggest that he is disloyal and bad. Such an attitude may be unconscious, but if put into words could be expressed, roughly, in some such phrases as these: the welfare and prosperity, the safety and security of the group into which I was born or adopted early in life is more important than the welfare, safety, security and even the lives of all the rest of the people in the world. This is an attitude that is widely held. "My loyalty belongs to my group" was the thinking and feeling of our ancestors. But such an attitude has become, like many others, exceedingly dangerous; a new one must replace it.

The human race is now in jeopardy. It is, of course, arguable how many survivors there would be if we should have a third world war. Before he died, Einstein guessed that 25 per cent of the human race might conceivably survive a third world war. This estimate is now generally regarded as grossly optimistic because, when Einstein made that statement, the H-bomb had not been developed to its present degree of efficiency, nor was biological and chemical warfare as threatening as it is now.

There are a great many world problems awaiting solution about which we are hardly doing anything now, though they threaten the very survival of the human race since they are likely to produce a fighting war. One of these is the extremely pressing problem of food. Two-thirds of the children born today, tomorrow, this year or next, will be starving when they are born, starving all their lives. Because of food shortages there is no prospect at present that more than half the people of the world will be able to be reasonably healthy. Yet very little is being done. It is true that countries like Canada will sell wheat to anybody that can afford to buy but we have not been particularly generous about providing wheat for people just because they are hungry. The United Nations Food and Agricultural Organization is in the process of developing a programme to help eradicate this widespread starvation; they hope to receive a great deal of money to do this. Some twelve years ago, it attempted to set up a World Food Council to design methods by which food could be distributed on a world-wide basis but it was voted down because the nations of the world were not ready for it. Now, again, a new effort has begun. Its success will depend entirely on how much money we in Canada, and people like ourselves, will provide, how much food we will be willing to give to the Food and Agricultural Organization for planned distribution, how much help we will send to people in other parts of the world to increase their ability to grow food. All this will require a lot of money. However, the necessity is overwhelmingly great. We should meet it whatever the cost.

Hunger is not new in the world; indeed, in many parts of the world, it has always been taken for granted that many people would regularly die of starvation or exposure. Until recently, there has also been universal resignation to that fact. But now people are no longer resigned to starvation for themselves or for their children: they know it is not necessary. They know that it can be controlled, that food can be provided, if the peoples of the world exert themselves. The hunger of the world has thus produced a degree of danger that has never before existed. Men are no longer willing to starve.

Another of the great problems of the world about which we are doing practically nothing is the frightening explosion of population. This is not a problem of the future; it confronts us now. The United Nations Population Commission has made some thoroughly disturbing statements. It has said that the population of the world will double in the next forty years—which is to say that we shall add more people to our total numbers in the world in the next forty years, than we have done in the previous two hundred thousand years! This problem is complicating every other difficulty facing the human race. Some countries, Mexico for example, will double their population in twenty years. The economic and social effects of such a growth of population can hardly be imagined. There is no probability that sufficient food, housing, or any of the simple amenities will be available to cope with them.

Still another great problem is the disparity in the distribution of natural resources. The shocking fact is that North America is still using up now, as it has for years, about half of the world's total production from irreplaceable natural resources. It is not possible for people in other parts of the world to have anything like such a share of the world's resources. North America is known to be the most wasteful part of the world—utterly reckless in the destruction of material which could be used to advantage by many people in many parts of the world. It is quite commonly believed by people in southeast Asia and in Africa that numbers of people comparable to those now living in North America could thrive, in what they would regard as luxury, on the garbage dumps of our continent. In fact this is nearly true, because people live on astonishingly small amounts in other parts of the world: here, too, is a matter that must be looked at in the near future. However, there is no prospect that North America can, even in ten years from now, continue to enjoy any such proportion of the world's natural resources. Yet we are doing little or nothing to make reasonable arrangements for coping with this eventuality.

Security, of course, is another pressing problem. It is obvious, as we have been seeing, that our old methods simply do not work, that national armament is an obsolete concept because it can no longer defend us from death. But we are very reluctant to take the next appropriate steps, despite the fact that these are the kind of steps that were taken by our ancestors, for instance in Canada and in the United States, when the provinces of Canada and the colonies amalgamated and gave up some of their sovereignty and invested in a larger authority. The time has come to recognize that national sovereignty is no longer defensible; it has lost its validity. As far as can be seen now, we can have security only by having a police force which will be available to enforce world law. We have submitted ourselves to law within national boundaries, but must we stop there? Must we not learn to submit ourselves to law on a world basis? We may talk hopefully about disarmament, but it is not likely that we will achieve any appreciable or valuable degree of disarmament until we have a world police force. Never in human history have men disarmed before they had policemen or sheriffs to provide local protection. There is no likelihood now that we will disarm and reduce international tensions until we do have some sort of world police force to enforce world law. We are, of course, very reluctant to do this because this disturbs our loyalties—loyalties that were appropriate for our ancestors, but which are not appropriate for us in our new kind of world.

One can go on and on pointing to various problems which require our thought and attention, but nothing will really be done about them until enough people are willing to pay the price, a price that imposes some individual discomfort. In the first place, as we mentioned, there is the discomfort of thinking. Most of us have been taught in infancy not to think, but only to accept whatever our parents believed about everything. It becomes very necessary to question such old patterns. The mere fact that my father believed something is not sufficient reason for my believing it. Had I been born even just in the house next door, I would have been subjected to a different set of certainties. There is no obligation on the human race or any part of it to submit to that sort of accident; besides, it is much too dangerous. We are going to have to learn to think independently of the attitudes of our ancestors in relation to these new situations and surely most of all in relation to security.

Within reach of every idividual who is reasonably intelligent and mature is some part of the answer to these great problems. The solutions are within our reach in our homes and schools, our businesses and our churches. Nothing effective is going to be done until enough individuals accept their responsibility and determine to act. A great many people, feeling that something should be done, will immediately say: "I would like to get a job in the United Nations and thus do something significant!" But the United Nations is not being allowed to do significant things, and will not be, until enough people who have mature attitudes stay at home and see that those attitudes permeate their own cultures, and eventually reach their governments. This is our problem, our responsibility, and the open choice which is ours.

The ethic of these attitudes that I have been suggesting may not reflect the ethic of the attitudes of our ancestors, or even of our parents. Let us, however, remember that the great men of the past—all the great prophets in the economic, social, legal, political, or religious fields—were, in their time and place, rebels against the orthodoxies into which they were born. They were people who exhorted their contemporaries to change their attitudes, to bring them up to the level of the knowledge available, and not go on blindly following the past. We do not do any of our great prophets a service by freezing their ideals as at the time of their death. Not one of them would agree to that for they were all people who went on growing as long as they lived, and if they were alive now they would still be growing and adjusting to changed circumstances.

Loyalty, then, needs some reconsideration. Loyalty to principles that are still valid, but only on the basis of our own judgment, not on the basis of the patterns that have come to us from the past. If enough people come to recognize their true freedom of choice, and have the fortitude to exercise that freedom, to apply it as far as they can within their own situation, it may be that we can help human evolution to continue.

3 / The Ethical Goals of Modern Education

MURRAY G. ROSS

I begin by quoting a great philosopher on the question with which we are concerned: "Mankind are by no means agreed about the best things to be taught, whether we look to virtue or the best life. Neither is it clear whether education is more concerned with intellectual or with moral virtue. The existing practice is perplexing; no one knows on what principle we should proceed—should the useful in life, or should virtue, or should the higher knowledge, be the main aim of our training?"

It is not a modern philosopher or educator raising this relevant question, but Aristotle, speaking many centuries ago. But the same question is still being asked, and the same basic problem is still perplexing men. There are many who seem to say that the university (and I will confine myself largely to the university) is concerned solely with matters of the intellect (as if the intellect were a separate and unrelated entity possessed by man), and that matters of virtue or of goodness or of ethical conduct are personal matters which lie outside the province of the university. There are others who seem to believe that the primary function of the university is to prepare students for various professions in society, and that however important may be such theoretical questions as virtue and goodness, they have little relation to the real and practical world in which men must work and earn a living.

If you think I exaggerate, you should look carefully at trends in universities in North America. You will find, I believe, two developments of interest. One is the growing status of the physical sciences in the modern university, and the other is the increasing number of professional faculties. Now these are natural and appropriate developments in our society. But both of these developments give an emphasis and a focus to university education that make questions of goodness or virtue of secondary or tertiary importance. Indeed, it is possible for a student to go from high school to any one of many universities and, if he is specializing in science to take only science courses, or if he is studying a profession to take only courses related to the profession. These developments would be less important—since one's course work is only a part of university education—if it were not for the fact that they influence the whole structure and character of the university. And this influence, while it does not necessarily depreciate ethics or philosophy or religion, none the less tends to exclude effective consideration of such matters by giving priority to other topics, which are made to appear to be of more immediate or more practical concern.

My own view is that these developments are extremely unfortunate. It is often said that the purpose of the university is to discover and to disseminate knowledge. But it can hardly stop there. "Knowledge grows but wisdom lingers," says the sage, and it is surely the responsibility of the university itself to use, and to help its students to use, knowledge in the treating of the great and difficult problems of life. It is not sufficient that men be trained at the university to cut holes in a mountain, or in a tooth, or in an abdomen, if they have not also been led to contemplate the nature of their own being, or the meaning of their own behaviour.

I believe that, as one of its primary functions, the university must constantly engage in the task of seeking to know and understand the nature of truth and goodness, and should, therefore, be engaged in endless debate and discussion of all questions relevant to this search. Although it is not the business of the university to become involved in the intricacies of establishing political policies, or ethical goals for individuals, it is surely the task of those in the university to encourage and stimulate, by their own questions and by discussion, consideration of broad social goals which may give focus and purpose to society and to the members of society. As Walter Lippmann said:

... if civilization is to be coherent and confident it must be known in that civilization what its ideals are. There must exist in the form of clearly available ideas an understanding of what the fulfilment of the promise of that civilization might mean, an imaginative conception of the good at which it might, and, if it is to flourish, at which it must aim. That knowledge, though no one has it perfectly, and though relatively few have it at all, is the principle of all order and certainty in the life of that people. By it they can clarify the practical conduct of life in some measure, and add immeasurably to its dignity.

No institution in our society is as well equipped as is the university to create a *milieu* in which such matters may be examined. For the university is inhabited by men who are part of society, yet, in a sense, work apart from it. They are made free in and by the university to pursue their study of society and to speculate about the nature of goodness. They thus have social support for their primary obligation—which is the pursuit of truth.

Besides the provision of an environment in which long-range problems of moral behaviour may be considered, the university has still another obligation. This I believe to be the obligation to involve each of her sons (that is, every one of her students) in a search for personal answers to the fundamental questions of life. The university's task is not, of course, to *provide* the answers, but to expose the student to the questions, to provide him with some resources which he may bring to bear on these questions, and, above all, to encourage him to use his own intelligence in confronting ethical problems.

The university should, therefore, be involved in providing those ingredients essential for a developing or maturing system of philosophy or ethics. The university is also involved in disseminating knowledge and in teaching students to think—to utilize knowledge. The great weakness today is that some universities ignore these functions, and some perform them inadequately. They assume that students will relate and integrate fragmented knowledge, that students will discover naturally the great questions with which men have been confronted throughout the ages, that students will themselves readily find the motivation to read and speculate and talk about the nature of beauty and justice and goodness. It is my experience that this does not always happen—even among students in the Faculty of Arts, let alone in the professional faculties. The situation could be improved by requiring all students to study philosophy and ethics at appropriate points in their university curriculum, but much more is required. The very *ethos* of the university must be such that not only is discussion and debate about fundamental problems of life and living tolerated, it is actually encouraged, nourished, and guided. When this happens, the university is engaged in its real business: it is not merely turning up fragments of knowledge, not just teaching students how to perform professional functions—it is a community, united by a common desire to understand man and his destiny.

II

I want to turn now to a more detailed description of the implications of this view of a university. A system of ethics involves, I believe, some understanding of ourselves, some understanding of the society of which we are members, and a ceaseless search for a rational way of life. These are not, of course, separate and distinct enterprises, but are related, and overlapping. I will discuss them separately, however, both to emphasize the nature of each, and to illustrate the fact that if these are prerequisites to the development of an ethical system, they are also the very matters which the university wishes to illuminate for members of the university and for society as a whole.

I say that ethics involves understanding of self because ethics assumes or calls for rational choice and behaviour by relatively mature individuals. And such behaviour is not possible for those who are unaware that the goals they pursue are selected for reasons quite different from the reasons they suppose. So much evil has been perpetrated in the name of goodness that this fact should be obvious to everyone. It is, as Dean Inge suggests, the kind of behaviour to be expected from those persons who fancy themselves attracted to God when they are really only repelled by man.

The wisdom and insight that come to us from Freud and those who followed him suggest the complex sources that motivate man in his behaviour. Not only is it extremely difficult to identify the real motives of behaviour, but man has become so skilful at rationalizing his behaviour that he can readily deceive both himself and his associates. The Puritan devotes himself to work and thrift because he believes this is God's way, although some observers might feel he merely follows the way to the greatest material rewards. (As Max Weber pointed out, the money the Protestant business man accumulates is proof to him that he has fulfilled his ethical duty.) The early liberals were in favour of freedom because freedom was essential to the dignity of man, although many have felt that some of these liberals sought freedom so that they would be free to build up their business empires. The parent or teacher punishes the child for "his own good," but some observers might see some such punishment as a way by which the teacher or parent releases some of his own deep, inner hostility.

One of the most revealing insights in respect of motive and behaviour is to be found in Erich Fromm's conception of selfishness and of "self-love." The popular opinion has been that these two were synonymous, but Fromm develops at some length, and in a most convincing manner, the theory that it is only the self-loving person who is capable of loving others. The person who knows and accepts his own self, and who is confident in his own self-evaluation, does not need others merely for psychic security, but is capable of loving others as he loves himself. On the other hand, Fromm suggests that a "selfish" person has no real self and no fondness for self, therefore he must constantly seek security in terms of conquests and power as compensation for his lack of "self-love." In other words, the selfish person is not interested in himself, but only in the evaluation of himself by others. He shines, as David Riesman suggests, in their reflected light—he is their satellite, even when he dominates them.

However one may regard these theories, one must admit the complexity of human motive. Understanding of human behaviour, and especially of one's own behaviour, is difficult indeed. But surely if our actions are to be ethical, we must make the effort to understand the forces which seem to push us in one direction or another. To be ethical requires, as I have suggested, that we be rational—and to be rational requires understanding of man in general, and of self in particular.

The degree to which understanding and intelligence and will can regulate and guide impulse and desire is a matter which has not been settled, and, indeed, may never be settled satisfactorily. At the moment, one's judgment on the matter reflects one's beliefs and faith rather than one's certain knowledge. But surely man is not simply the creature of his environment, past or present. Surely he has some capacity to regulate his life. It can be argued with justification that the degree to which he can regulate all or any part of his behaviour is itself determined by his past and present environment. But, given some intelligence and will, combined with a growing knowledge of human motive and increasing understanding of self, it seems probable that man's capacity to regulate his life can gradually be increased.

This is, of course, touchy and highly debatable ground. What does one say of the neurotically shy person? To suggest, as some do, that he should adjust to his condition—even, if necessary, avoid meeting new people, attending parties, or joining any gathering of people which might upset him—seems to me to be a negative and defeatist point of view. There are many types of shy people, I suppose: some have "adjusted to their condition" and live in isolation as much as possible; others, with varying degrees of effort and sacrifice, regulate or control their fears, and, while never finding it possible to relax and fully enjoy new people and new situations, none the less find a means of functioning relatively effectively in business and social situations; some, through knowledge and understanding and will, work through their problems and gradually find their shyness being reduced in intensity. My own view is that these kinds of adjustment represent stages from defeatism to control to understanding and maturity. And this is the direction of movement required by all of us if we are to be rational, ethical, mature people.

The essence of Freud's insight and message was that understanding would pave the way for rational action. It was lack of insight into oneself and one's nature that made for moral paralysis. Freud believed in integrity and in intelligence. His aim was to expose the infantile sources of many of the demands people make on themselves and on others, so that they might become free, or comparatively free, to choose their own way. All of us are bound or imprisoned in greater or lesser degree by our past experiences, some traces of which lie deeply buried in our unconscious. Freud's message is that we can only be free to deal with the present and the future as we learn to understand and come to terms with these pressures of the past.

I cannot leave this side of my discussion without saying that this is an area in which "a little knowledge is a dangerous thing," and in which many distortions have developed. A juvenile delinquent about whom I read recently explained his behaviour by saying he was a "mixed-up kid" and couldn't help doing what he did. We can use a little knowledge to excuse unethical behaviour of many kinds. One of Arthur Koestler's stories is, I think, relevant:

> Pythagoras, it is supposed, was drawing triangles in the sand. A friend came up and sat by him and Pythagoras said: "I don't know why I keep on drawing these triangles. They worry me and fascinate me." His friend asked shrewdly: "What is your relationship like with your wife?" Pythagoras looked a bit downcast, and mumbled that he feared her affections were straying. "Aha!" said his friend: "I now see why you can't keep your mind off those triangles." "I suppose you are right," said Pythagoras. He then got up and did nothing further about developing his theorem! Many a decent man has wanted to do something worthwhile but has had his confidence undermined by irrelevant remarks like: "You only do it because you unconsciously need approval"—as if his unconscious had anything to do with the worthwhileness of what he intended.

This is surely a distortion of what is possible for man. I do not deny that there is much talk that is confusing and damaging. But to suggest that one would be less creative, less generous, less capable, if one understood oneself and one's motives is to depreciate the function of knowledge and intelligence. To suggest that we can progress without self-knowledge is to admit, as Lawrence Kubie suggests, that we can have no adults but only aging children.

Ethical behaviour, therefore, requires some knowledge of human nature, of its drives and desires, of its complexity and its adaptive capacity. Ethical behaviour requires, particularly, some understanding of self and its unique nature. For without such knowledge and understanding, our choices may well be made, not as rational and mature men, but as well-conditioned animals responding with a predictable reaction to any given stimulus. It is not given to any of us to understand ourselves or others fully, but the whole thrust of the university is towards bringing ever larger areas of behaviour under intelligent direction. One must admit that modern society, with its devotion to the machine, seems to be moving in the opposite direction, but this is a trend which must be opposed by all men of goodwill and intelligence. Our search for understanding of self must be continuous, so that the ethical choices we make may ever more nearly approximate rational and intelligent decisions.

III

I would suggest, secondly, that a man who seeks to behave rationally must have some understanding of social structure and social forces, and the ways in which these tend to shape and condition both thought and behaviour.

It has frequently been said that there is no single human act which we would judge "good" in our culture which would not be judged "bad" in another culture. This is perhaps less true today as the world grows smaller, polygamy less popular, and Flanders and Swann are heard to sing in the four corners of the earth "Eatin' People is Wrong." But the overriding influence of our culture on behaviour is a fact now widely recognized, even though most of us operate as if this were not the case. Of course, it is not easy to see the social forces that mould our behaviour, although once someone identifies them for us, we recognize their potency at once. "The Cult of

Fun," about which Dr. Martha Wolfenstein writes, is a case in point. She suggests that in our society we have come to believe that, whatever else it may be, life *must* be fun: we must have *fun* with the baby, with the children, with our friends. If we don't have "fun" in a situation which calls for "fun"—and the number of such situations is increasing rapidly —there must be something the matter with us. I quote from Dr. Wolfenstein:

> Not having fun is not merely an occasion for regret, but involves a loss of self-esteem. I ask myself: What is wrong with me that I am not having fun? To admit that one did not have fun when one was expected to, arouses feelings of shame. Where formerly it might have been thought that a young woman who went out a great deal might be doing wrong, currently we would wonder what is wrong with a girl who is not going out. Fun and play have assumed a new obligatory aspect. While gratification of forbidden impulses traditionally aroused guilt, failure to have fun currently occasions lowered self-esteem. One is apt to feel inadequate, impotent, and also unwanted. One fears the pity of one's contemporaries rather than, as formerly, possible condemnation by moral authorities.

Let me give one additional example, from Moss Hart's *Act One*:

> Even in the long-ago days when I was growing up, the cult of "toughness" in American life was beginning to blossom and flower. The non-athletic boy, the youngster who liked to read or listen to music, who could not fight or was afraid to, or the boy who had some special interest that was strange or alien to the rest, like the theatre, in my case, was banished from the companionship of the others by the rules of the "tough" world that was already beginning to prevail.
> It is a mistake to believe that this cult of "toughness" was limited to the poor neighbourhood in which we lived. It had begun to pervade other levels of American life, and I suspect that today's bland dismissal of the intellectual and the over-whelming emphasis placed on the necessity of competing and of success are

due in part to the strange taboo we have set against that softness in ourselves which brings men closest to the angels. A nation of poets would be no more desirable than a nation of athletes, but I wonder if that toughness and competitiveness, which have become an ingrained part of our character as a people and a symbol of our way of life as a nation, are not a sign of weakness as well as of strength.

Here, then, are two cults in our society. We can hardly deny their existence, and we are forced, I believe, to admit their influence in our lives. My point is simply that a man who is seeking to live a rational life must be aware of these influences and not accept the resultant behaviour as "good" simply because it is a pattern of behaviour that prevails and is accepted in society at large, or by a subdivision of the society. Indeed, in other societies and cultures, the two cults I have mentioned would not be understood, or accepted.

I have been particularly impressed by the influence of induced attitude and behaviour in different cultures by recent visits to the Soviet Union and the People's Republic of China. In the Western world, we assume "our enemy" is the Soviet Union; in the U.S.S.R., the assumption is that the West is the "enemy." Many things in each culture—especially the official propaganda—support this belief, so that firm and fixed attitudes about "the enemy" develop, reinforce each other, and there thus emerge the most outlandish ideas of each other's behaviour. As a result, "we" in North America and "they" in the Soviet Union, because of the different cultural perceptions we have, draw almost opposite conclusions from every action taken by either side. The United States' military bases in Europe and Asia are a case in point. For us, these bases are essentially defensive—a means of protecting ourselves and our way of life. For the Russians, they are offensive bases, from which some day a huge attack on the Soviet Union will be launched. And just as we say "How can they possibly believe that about us?" so the Soviets said, when I stated some of our beliefs about *their* behaviour, "How can you think such things about us?"

What I am suggesting is that in every culture certain attitudes and behaviour patterns develop which we unconsciously "take over"; these become part of our daily life, operating almost like an unconscious mechanism to guide and direct what we say or do. If we define ethical behaviour as rational behaviour, we cannot accept such mechanistic direction of our lives as ethical, even though it produces words and actions that appear right and proper to our friends and neighbours. If I am to act towards the Soviet Union as an ethical person, I must think through to my own position in the matter. The final result of such thought may, none the less, be the popular, negative reaction to the Soviet Union; but it has at least discounted the *pressure* to be negative, and is now based on a determination to look objectively at the situation, to make judgments on the basis of the highest intellectual effort that can be brought to bear on the problem.

Within the general culture as a whole, there are also innumerable subcultures, one or more of which will inevitably influence our beliefs and values. Some of you will have read Dorothea Natwick's *We Happy Few*, which presents such an illuminating picture of the Harvard faculty, into which the heroine marries. The ideas, values, and behaviour of this group are clear and distinctive, and they influence the attitudes and the behaviour of every member. "For this group, everything is *'interesting,'* nothing is serious—nothing, that is, except the bitter rivalries for prestige and place. There is a terrible striving always to be *avant-garde*, to 'discover' Henry James, T. S. Eliot, Melville, or the more obscure English poets. There is a standing rule for admission to the 'happy few' who call themselves 'The Little Group': *never to be taken in by any person, idea or emotion.*" This subculture, which developed almost apart from any single individual, conditions, if not directs, the behaviour of every single member of the group.

There are innumerable studies to suggest very different attitudes and patterns of behaviour among various subgroups in our society. There are different values placed, for example, on education, on money-making, on skin pigmentation, and so on. There are different attitudes to crime, sickness, family-size. All this, of course, we know, but many of us seem to know it only vaguely and ineffectively.

Without going into further detail, it is perhaps sufficient to say that, for many of us, what we say and do is less the result of rational thought than of responsiveness to certain patterns of belief and action characteristic of the society and sub-cultures to which we belong. Again, I would say that if ethical behaviour is rational behaviour, it requires us to understand the pressures to which we are subjected, and to bring these under control to as great a degree as is possible, so that our attitudes and behaviour may reflect what we ourselves truly believe to be "right" and "good" behaviour.

IV

A third requirement for ethical behaviour is that we be engaged in a ceaseless search for goodness, both as an ideal and as a guiding and directing force in our lives. Most of us, of course, inherit ideas and beliefs which we perpetuate with little effectiveness and without satisfaction. As Lippmann suggests, "Men are choked with the debris of dead notions in which they are unable to believe and unwilling to disbelieve. The result is a frustration of the inner life..." which will persist as long as man relies merely on the past and refuses to confront the great questions of life with the new knowledge available to him.

The truth of this assertion was revealed to me several years ago when I undertook a study of the religious attitudes and beliefs of young people in the United States. The findings of this study have been published under the title *Religious Beliefs of Youth,* and although there is a great temptation to discuss this subject in detail, I will restrict myself to the major theme. Perhaps I can summarize best by quoting Professor Gordon Allport, of Harvard University, who wrote the "Introduction" to the book. He summarized its findings thus:

> Modern youth has strong religious inclinations and gives at least verbal assent to the religious traditions of his culture. At the same time, he is passive in his religious life, and basically confused about the place of religion in his own personality and in society at large.... Echoes of childhood fears, of superstition, of immaturity, continually appear in these findings. Even if they are churchgoers, most young people feel detached from the institutions of religion. Like banks and museums, they are regarded as possessions of the older generation, not really a concern of youth.... In reading this book, one is struck by a central paradox. It appears that belief in God is almost universal, prayer is a widespread practice, there is a prevailing friendly estimate of the church.... At the same time, there is a ghostly quality about these beliefs. They seem like heirlooms that fit badly into a modern dwelling. The task of integrating the values of religion with the present needs of daily life is one that very few youths seem able to carry through. Evidence suggests that in not more than a fifth of the cases can one find an integrated religious sentiment at work, binding parts of the personality into a functioning unity.... For most youth, religion in large part seems like a remote if pleasant memory. What it teaches is unclear and its bearing on present activities is dim. To borrow Renan's phrase, its nostalgic quality is like the perfume from an empty vase.

The reason why this state of religion has developed among youth is that a given body of dogma has been impressed or forced upon or taught to children and young people in such a way that they have never since felt called upon to question its basic assumptions. My colleague, Professor Seeley, has pointed out that religion has generally been passed on to children in the same way, but that in other periods of history it was passed on successfully. Why are traditional methods ineffective today? The reason is, as he points out, that the social situation has changed, and is changing, at an accelerated rate. Many of the old landmarks are gone; new guideposts can only be found by those willing to be venturesome and to make the effort. There are few of these latter, and the result is a body of "dead notions" in which we fear to disbelieve, but in which we are unable to believe. Most young people reach this point; and, if maintained, it is a crippling, if not paralyzing, attitude to life. The body of dogma lies as an undigested mass, accepted—even revered—but largely meaningless, and certainly ineffective as a motivating force in life.

One aspect of the study (which was not published because the sample upon which my conclusions were based was too small, and because of the difficulty in being precise about such intangible factors) dealt with people who did have a meaningful belief which was clearly an integral part of their life. I was much interested in trying to discover what, if any, common factors were present among the people who had such a faith. Although the sample was small, the people were from a wide variety of backgrounds. There were in this group devout Catholics, a Quaker, a Unitarian, an agnostic, a number of orthodox Protestant church members, and several members of evangelistic sects. What could possibly be common to the members of such a heterogeneous group? The only common thread that I could find was that in almost every case that person had been through a period of doubt and searching before finding the faith or philosophy that now gave meaning and purpose to his life.

This study forced upon me the conclusion that a faith that has never been questioned may be, or will be, a faith that has little meaning or influence in life. It seemed clear to me that religious leaders—indeed, all educators—should, instead of instructing, training, indoctrinating youth, be encouraging youth to question and to search. In my view, the only way that an individual can find faith, purpose, and meaning in life is to discover for himself that which seems worth believing in, and giving loyalty to. To accept, simply, the views of others, means, inevitably (to paraphrase Renan) that even though there may be some odour of perfume present, the vase is empty—there are really no flowers! It may be, of course, that the search will bring acceptance of, and devotion to, the views of the church, or of the synagogue, or of Aldous Huxley, or of Lord Russell. But if these views are to be meaningful to the individual, he must have searched, questioned, and discovered for himself that these beliefs *are* compelling for him.

v

I come now to the question of what relation exists between ethics and education. The answer must already be obvious.

A system of ethics requires a rational approach to the problems of life and living. It requires that we undertake a consistent search for answers to life's difficult questions so that we may be helped in finding the "good life"; it requires that we seek constantly to achieve greater understanding of ourselves and the social forces that impinge upon us; it requires that we strive ceaselessly to make our thoughts and actions harmonious.

As I have already suggested, the university has two responsibilities in this respect. One is that of unending enquiry. The enquiry goes on because it *has* to go on. The enquiry may cease in society at large because of weariness of mind and body, and because sterility is there. But as long as the vitality of the university is unimpaired, we must agree with Mr. Whitehead that "it belongs to the self-respect of intellect to pursue every tangle of thought to its final unravelment." This is one of the great functions of the university, and, so long as it pursues this function, it serves both as a symbol of man's search for truth and as a source of inspiration and knowledge to men as they strive individually to find their own ethical system.

The university is also dedicated to helping each of its students to meet the very requirements I have emphasized as being essential for a system of ethics: to increase understanding of self, to develop awareness of cultural forces, to engage upon a search for compelling beliefs.

I came across, the other day, an examination paper in philosophy I had written in 1934. The major part of the paper required discussion of the following statements:

1. We cannot judge an act by its consequences because we never know all its consequences.
2. We cannot judge an act by its motive because our motives are not under our control.
3. There is no connection between doing what is right and bringing into being what is good except that doing what is right is itself good when I do it because I think it right.
4. Is not duty opposed to desire or is there a desire to do one's duty? If so, is it one desire among others?
5. Conscience in the individual is just the consciousness of custom and group approval.
6. Conscience represents the constraint or impulsion of mass elements in the margin or fringe of consciousness rather than the discernment of the focus of our minds.
7. Conscience is just intelligent deliberation or judgment applied to conduct.

My own answers then, I now believe, were not particularly good, but this is much less important than the fact that, at an early date, I was engaged by a stimulating professor and congenial fellow-students in lengthy discussion and debate about such questions as I have reported. One cannot have such an experience and not be helped to speculate about the meaning of goodness, and the nature and direction of one's behaviour.

For me, such speculation is an essential part of university education. There is a great danger that university education will become vocational education; the growth of professional faculties into which one moves directly from high school is one indication of this danger. Another "straw in the wind" is that one out of every eight university students in the United States is now studying Business, and, although I have no objection to Business, nor to Pharmacy, nor to Engineering, I do believe that, in the university, the type of emphasis in many professional faculties prohibits the kind of education I have been talking about. The emphasis in such faculties is on vocation. The real business of the university is man.

Part Two: Group Relations

MORDECAI W. JOHNSON

LOUIS FINE

THOMAS M. EBERLEE

4 / The Moral Challenge of Underdeveloped Peoples

MORDECAI W. JOHNSON

My approach to this paper has been determined by my strong conviction that it is important for the life or death of our Western civilization that we look at the human rights of the underdeveloped peoples of Africa, Asia, and South America. Here are the areas which are likely to be decisive for us in the dangerous contest which we are now engaged in with the Communist world.

From the point of view of the Soviet Union, I think, the first phase of their struggle with us has reached a favourable conclusion, and they are now prepared to enter the second stage the end of which they believe will see them as the dominant power in the coming unification—political, economic, and moral—of the modern world. As the result of the first phase of this struggle, in their view, they have succeeded in the acquisition and effective consolidation of a billion followers, and in the control of a fourth of the landed surface of the earth—a surface so situated and so filled with valuable resources that it is possible for them to demonstrate Communist development in a fashion increasingly persuasive to all mankind; from it, as their base of operations, they can steadily and rapidly gather increasing numbers of supporters all over the world. The second phase of their struggle with us involves the projection of their economic purposes into the world of underdeveloped peoples in Africa, Asia, and South America. This phase has already begun. In this economic offensive we shall confront the central purposes of the Soviet Union and her allies, and we shall meet, I believe, the most powerful opposition of ideas, the most vigorously intelligent and revolutionary handling of the economic and spiritual factors of life that any group of people in the world has ever faced. We must meet that onslaught of ideas, of political, economic, and organizational power with a vigorous readjustment of our lives, or we shall fall from our long-standing position of privilege in the world and possibly lose any power to control the trend of history for years to come. But if we do meet the challenge boldly, realizing from the beginning that it will involve great decisions and the maximum use of all our powers, we may be able to pursue a course of action which will lift our democratic life to a level of efficient functioning higher than we have ever known before, and give us a radiant power over the lives and affections of men around the world such as we have not had in five hundred years.

Of the nearly three billion human beings in this world, there are one billion, two hundred million in Asia, Africa, and South America among whom the average scale of living is under a hundred dollars per capita per year. These people are living in a primarily agricultural civilization, and a very poor type of agriculture at that. They are living in countries in which there is very little industry to supplement agriculture. Practically all of them are impoverished in scientific and technical intelligence. There are, for the most part, no governmental personnel of modern political and scientific training who are prepared to make a wise and well co-ordinated use of scientific and technical plans and projections.

Eight hundred million of these people are living on the borders of the Soviet Union and of China, and so do not have to cross water to reach them.

All these eight hundred million people living close to the Communist nations are black and brown and yellow Asiatics who in times past have suffered at the hands of the peoples whom we represent, and who have some fear of us. The people in Africa and South America have had the same kind of painful relations with the leading nations of the West—Africa perhaps having suffered more than any others—and are known to have the same fearful concern. These are the people whom the Communists are approaching. We need to be realistically aware of their central purpose as they move out among the underdeveloped peoples, and we need to be very careful lest we underestimate the power of that purpose.

Causes which involve a terrible struggle, with many people on both sides, are never all good and never all evil, but are a mixture of both, each with a varying degree of relevancy to the struggle itself. It is an understandable human weakness that in such cases we all tend to concentrate our attention and our public utterances upon the evil and dangerous elements in the life and purposes of our enemies, and upon the good and salutary elements in our own life and purposes. However effective such measures may be for the temporary preservation of internal unity and morale, their accuracy, soundness, and wisdom are open to doubt and may lead us to under-estimate the real power of our enemy and to overestimate our own power. It is always a good thing that there be realists among us who insist upon weighing the good and the powerful things in our enemy's purposes and conduct and that we re-estimate ourselves from time to time with a humility that is determined to see the evil in our purposes and the weaknesses in our conduct.

Up to this time we have tended to look at the totalitarian side of our enemy's organization and upon his military and subversive aggression; and we have been facing him primarily with military power and counter subversion. We have paid little or no attention to the central focus of what he is about in the world. Now we must look at that central focus and, if we are wise, we will not allow our emotions of revulsion to prevent us from appraising it on the level represented by its highest and most intelligent and pure-hearted devotees. When we make this effort sincerely we can see that the central focus of the Communist movement is a simple and great faith: that the scientific, technical, and organizational intelligence at the disposal of modern man is sufficiently resourceful to overcome entirely the struggle for existence that now goes on among men throughout the world, to do away with poverty, squalor, disease, premature death, and ignorance, and to lay the foundation for a great society in which culture of every kind will be available to all human beings, provided only that the working people of the world can find leaders who love them enough to organize their energies for these purposes. The Communist party, its members and adherents believe, is the provider of this responsible leadership, and is now on its way to giving the working people of the world, of every race and creed and colour, the effective leadership and the organized activity which, they think, will certainly bring victory over poverty and squalor, disease, ignorance and early death.

These people hold this faith with a passion never exceeded by any movement in the world except early Christianity. They are responding to it every day and every hour with an enthusiasm which is nothing short of remarkable. On the ground of Russia and on Chinese soil they have had achievements of one kind or another which have astonished us. And now they are approaching the underdeveloped peoples of the world with an immense evangelistic eagerness.

The Soviet Union and her associated Communist countries are approaching these underdeveloped peoples simultaneously in Asia, Africa, and South America with simple and very relevant words like these: "Here we come to you from among those who, like yourself, have suffered. We are willing to help you, if you desire it, in a study of the land, mineral, and other natural resources of your country so as to prepare a

Moral Challenge of Underdeveloped Peoples / 53

programme of economic development which will enable your people to overcome poverty, squalor, disease, and premature death—in short to overcome the struggle for existence in such a way as to lay the foundation for a life of prosperity and growing culture for all of you. We are willing to come to show you how to treble and quadruple your agricultural production, to supplement your agriculture with the industries which we will show you how to establish, to lend you scientific and technical personnel, if need be, while we help you train your own young men and women for the work. We are prepared to lend you organizational leaders who know how to co-ordinate agricultural, industrial, and political work, and to help you to train your own leaders for this purpose. We are prepared to lend you needed tools and machinery or to lend you credit for purchasing them. If need be, we shall be glad to lend you money at rates so low that you will see in an unequivocally clear manner that we are not trying to make a profit from you. We are prepared to devote ourselves to this task for months and years solely because we believe that there is in you the same power to conquer the struggle for existence in your country as we have done in Russia and elsewhere, and we want to have the joy of seeing you do that."

In the pursuit of these aims, the Communists have committed themselves to what is, in effect, a radical universal ethics. They have specifically stated that they are not trying to organize the white people of the world to accomplish their purposes, but are trying to unite all the working people of the world, including all races, all colours, all creeds, all cultures, in a great common effort. They have, therefore, combined an economic objective fundamentally essential to the human race with their radical universal ethics. It is a formidable combination. I wish to emphasize that their purpose is not stated in the language of benevolent helpfulness, with its condescending pledges of 1 per cent, 2 per cent, 3 per cent of income. It is a radical purpose to effect such a widespread conquest of poverty as to deliver human beings everywhere from the anxiety and fear connected with poverty and to lay a world-wide foundation for brotherhood in economic security and cultural opportunity. It is to be emphasized also that it is their purpose to effect the conquest of poverty in every particular by organizational procedures which bring the full fruits of labour directly to the support of all who labour with their hands and with their minds, and thus greatly to reduce the time span between action and its effect on the people concerned.

We are confronting an immense antagonist, with a great objective that is relevant to all human life. He is pursuing that objective with a mighty and indefatigable passion. He is making progress with the underdeveloped peoples in Asia, Africa, and South America, and is making outstandingly significant political progress in the United Nations.

No small part of his progress in these areas has been facilitated by Western historical weaknesses, and by our present injurious habits and our blundering international conduct.

Nearly all the one billion, two hundred million underdeveloped peoples whom the Communists are now approaching have at one time or another come under our domination, as the result of what Toynbee describes as five hundred years of our aggression against them. During those years we have attacked and conquered nearly all of them; we have exploited their natural resources in a manner which they consider to have been unjust, and we have often segregated and humiliated them on the land of their fathers and in the presence of the graves of their mothers. They remember these things and in this hour when they are called upon to choose between us and the Soviet Union, there is in their hearts a fear of us which they cannot easily erase.

Although we have produced and developed democratic governmental institutions for ourselves, we have made no serious efforts to build these institutions up among the underdeveloped peoples. In fact, in relation to a very wide area of their lives we have been content to confine governmental officials to the bare purpose of maintaining order while we have devoted our attention primarily to the development and exploitation of their valuable natural resources. These natural resources, in Asia, Africa, and South America we have developed with all the scientific and technical skills at our command, not for the advancement of the native people concerned, but to build an immense wealth for ourselves. On the whole, we have put an amount of money at their disposal so low as to be shameful. We have segregated and humiliated them in public institutions, and we have done so according to an explicitly announced and implemented conception of their inferiority to us and hence their unworthiness of any treatment even approximating the thoughtful social concern that we have been accustomed to give to our own citizens.

When they look at the marvellous effects of scientific and technical intelligence upon our standards of living in the Western world they know that we had it in our power to transmit this intelligence to them and to their children long ago, but that we deliberately did not do so. They know, therefore, that the difference between their average standard of living of less than one hundred dollars per capita a year and our Western standard of living rising as high as two thousand dollars, is not due solely to themselves, but has been also the result of a contemptuous act of the will on our part maintained over years and years.

We are further harmed by injurious practices which have descended from the colonial system and which we have not yet been able to stop; indeed, we are divided in mind as to whether we intend to stop them. The underdeveloped people of the world have only to look at Africa to see how divided our minds are. On the one hand we see the British Empire setting India free and, one by one, freeing Ghana, Nigeria, and others from the colonial yoke and inviting them in their freedom back into the British Commonwealth as partners. On the other hand we see South Africa determinedly maintaining a segregated system of life which excludes the African peoples from all the major political, economic, and public service benefits of a civilization they helped to produce by years and years of labour. On the one hand we saw the Belgian nation going through the procedures of granting political freedom to the Congo. On the other hand we see nationals of that same country splitting asunder the land they freed in a tragic effort to hold onto the rich economic gains they won from the territory during the years they held the Congo in subjection.

Thus far the nations of the West who co-operatively developed the great military programme of the NATO powers, and magnificently carried out the Marshall Plan, have not even approached an agreement to liquidate thoroughly the last remnants of the colonial system and to make the rich natural resources of Africa effectively available for development by the African people themselves, although it is clearly in their power to do both.

Nobody can look at Africa and not realize that we are divided in our minds and that we have as yet been unable to summon either the political or the moral power to overcome that division. The same indecision operating in Africa operates also in the United States, the leader of the Western world.

On the one hand we see the impressive decisions of the Supreme Court of the United States seeking to overcome segregation in education and public facilities, and the President of the United States and his cabinet officers seeking to use their power to implement these objectives. On the other hand we see Congress both morally and politically powerless to legislate effectually to these ends, and the existence of a widespread and highly successful effort to delay obedience to and to frustrate the effectiveness of the laws that exist. On the one hand we see the President working long and hard to bring into existence a comprehensive programme of economic aid for Central and South America, for Asia and for Africa, supported by substantially increased appropriations and the power to make long-term financial commitments. On the other hand we see a determined coalition of segregationist and Northern and Western economizers delaying the passage of the measure, clipping and reducing the appropriation to annual droplets—all of which tends to throw doubt into the minds of proposed recipients everywhere regarding the stability and continuity of our purpose.

What is the result of all these evidences of our indecision? We have yielded to the Communist powers and the neutral powers the initiative and the responsibility of stimulating the United Nations to accelerate the liquidation of colonialism and we have raised in the minds of the still unfree and of the still underdeveloped peoples the most serious questions about the sincerity of our political and economic purposes.

May I say to you again, we have as yet been unable to formulate any world-encircling concept to replace the colonial system to which we have been devoted for some five hundred years and which is now fallen. The British do indeed have such a concept and have made some significant progress with it, but the NATO powers as a group have not embraced it or anything resembling it. What greater universal idea do we now have that we can offer these underdeveloped peoples of Asia, Africa, and South America: an idea of a new world of which they can be members just as we, in which they can be respected just as we, in which they can move freely out of their own spontaneous enthusiasm just as we? I suggest to you that we do not yet have one. There are no great words coming from us today regarding the city that hath foundations made for the whole human race of one blood; and, because we do not have such a concept, we are in some difficulty in approaching Asiatics and Africans and South Americans.

We in the Western world appear, then, to have at present no moral or political power to give unequivocal expression to a sincere purpose to liquidate as rapidly as possible the existing remnants of the colonial system. It is perfectly clear that we have not agreed upon any programme; that we are merely permitting individually large and small nations to follow their own national economic interests to such steps of liquidation as may seem acceptable to them; and that we are allowing them to take their time to do it, whatever may be the cost in suffering to the people under their domination. Indeed in the last two hundred years we did not have any interest in using our scientific and technical intelligence and our great organizing ability to make the immense natural resources of Africa, Asia, and South America available for the development of a modern civilized life for their own native people. We were unconcerned about their welfare to such an extent that we have left them today with a standard of life far below any appreciable approximation of a level adequate for good health. We really never began to have in mind any approximation to a large constructive economic programme until we were obliged to confront the programme of the Communists. Even then the programme which we have offered was for a long time not primarily an economic programme designed to be greatly helpful to the development of those peoples for their own sake, but an accessory to our military programme and a part of our defence. We see the Communists moving in to places like Guinea and Cuba and Egypt with far-reaching programmes of land reform, rapid development of industrial enterprises, and so on, but we still are moving defensively and in a very limited way. In the United States we are devoting to the whole problem less than half our annual expenditure for alcoholic beverages and the sum for foreign aid would be nothing compared with our combined bill for alcohol and tobacco.

It is not sufficient to emphasize that, under these circumstances, we are likely to fail in our effort to stop the growth of Communism in these countries. There is more to be said. If we see ourselves failing in this important area, our pride will not be able to endure it. We shall find ourselves constrained almost irresistibly to fight it out, rather than to be humiliated in this way. We shall then find ourselves in a position that we now hardly begin to realize: that we are in a war which has the possibility of destroying both the Communist powers and ourselves. This conclusion does not bring out the full significance of the catastrophe; we will have brought about this result at a time when the whole world has been brought into a physical unity by our activities as a world power; and when the world was eagerly hungering for this physical unity to be transformed into a political, economic and spiritual unity of a pluralistic nature in which, for the first time in history, its diverse peoples could begin, co-operatively, to promote those great common objectives which now appear so important for all mankind. The tragedy which we will have caused is that we will have destroyed the two groups, either of which had sufficient resources to be able to develop into one of the leaders of a world-wide co-operative union.

The questions which arise about the nature and sincerity of our purpose in the Western world in the disappointed and eager hearts of the underdeveloped peoples are not their questions merely. They are the questions which the eternal God of history is asking of us. They are moral questions of the deepest and most fundamental importance. It is clear that we have not yet explicitly answered them. If we have any respect for the greatest moral traditions which belong to us and any rational hope left in us for that unity for which the world now hungers, these are questions which we must answer. They might be phrased as follows:

1. Do you leaders of the economic and political life of the United States and the North Atlantic nations really believe in the unity of the human race?

2. Do you leaders of the economic and political life of the United States and the North Atlantic nations intend to use

the enormous powers at your disposal to do away with the remnants of the colonial system in Africa, Asia, and South America, and to deliver their people from the racial discrimination, segregation, and humiliation which have descended to them from that colonial system?

3. Do you leaders of the economic and political life of the United States and the North Atlantic nations intend to accept the moral responsibility that goes with your enormous scientific, technical, organizational, and productive genius to lay down, in your own way, a programme for the economic advancement of the people of this earth in such a way that the working men and women of the world as well as the working men and women of America and Europe can have a reasonable expectancy in this generation of overcoming the struggle for existence and of being able to feed, clothe, and house themselves and their children without killing one another? Or do you intend to use this power to dominate and control the earth and to confirm the subordination and anxiety and bitterness through which the world has been led during the last two hundred years?

There was once a man named Hitler who answered these questions in his own way, bluntly and categorically. To the first question, "Do you believe in the unity of the human race?" his answer was that God made no such thing as one family; that from the beginning God had only limited amounts of the best blood at His disposal; that He gave all but a little of that to the superior German people; that the greater portion of the rest He gave to the British; and that the remaining inhabitants of the human world were all but equal in their lack of it. His answer to the second question might be discerned from the praise he gave the British as he looked at what they were doing in South Africa and in other parts of their empire. He said that outside of the Germans themselves, the British were the only ones who knew how to deal with inferior people with the hardness that was necessary in order

Moral Challenge of Underdeveloped Peoples / 61

to keep the emotions from being engaged in a way to soften the will at a time when history required the will of superior people to be hard and merciless. It was utter folly, he thought, to believe that there were now or ever would be sufficient natural resources in the world to supply the needs of this immense population of inferior people who were cluttering up the earth. It was the duty, therefore, of all peoples of superior blood, notably Germans, and, with some reservations, Britons, to help themselves to such proportions of the land and natural resources of the world as they considered themselves to need, and then, without pity, to leave the vast masses of inferior people to take what they could get of the remaining land and resources. His shocking and horrible extermination of the Jewish people, in accordance with this immoral conception of human life, will be remembered with revulsion as long as humanity survives.

If Hitler were alive he would say that there is no need to ask us for an explicit answer to these questions because our deeds, for the last two hundred years at least, give ample evidence that we intend to keep on doing what we have been doing, namely, answering "No" to all of them. He would say that we do not believe in the unity of the human race. He would say that some races of the world are inherently superior to others, and by that inherent superiority have the right to subordinate and even completely exclude the inferior from basic rights characteristic of the lives of superior citizens; that we do not intend to liquidate all of the colonial system; and that if certain circumstances of history seem to constrain us to do so, we shall go as far as we are obliged to go, that we will delay moving as much as we can, and defeat the purpose altogether if we can. Finally, he would say that we do not accept the moral responsibility to develop any programme for economic progress on this earth; that our main business is to look after our own interest; that it is the business of other people to look after themselves; and that we are justified in helping them in their development only as far as our imperilled self-interest requires and only with such additional assistance as properly belongs in the realm of benevolence.

I do not believe this. I believe that we Western people are unable to forget the ideas which have come to us from the Bible; that we may drift away from our allegiance to them for a time, as in the decade just before the destruction of the slave system in America, but that their moral power is only slumbering in our bosoms. When the time of history is ripe, and the leader whom we need is pushed upon the platform by the movement of history to demand that we renew our allegiance to these great ideas, we have the capacity to rise from our moral slumbering and to answer him effectively. This we did in America when Abraham Lincoln called us. This we did when our great President Franklin Roosevelt called us. This we will do again if we are called in this crisis by a leader of authentic moral power.

When that leader calls—and we pray that he will call—I believe that he will declare certain things to be our necessary objectives in these times. He will want, first of all, an immediate cessation from war and the threat of war. He will believe that this kind of peace is possible now and he will lead us to it. He will want peace with Russia and Communism, and by this he will mean not only a peaceful coexistence while we move ahead in the struggle, but a peace which grows out of determined and effective objectives mutually agreed upon.

He will want peace with Russia and Communism in such a way as to preserve the institutions and practices of freedom which are the basic achievements and heritage of the Western world and to enhance these institutions and practices of freedom.

Our leader will be as fully aware of the evil in Communistic practices as we are, and will not have us relax our defences against it, but he will teach us to repudiate entirely the notion that everything about Russia is evil. His moral instincts will tell him that it is not true and that if we continue to insist upon it as being true, we shall have closed off any pathway to peace except by the defeat of our enemy in war and will be moving toward that war with relentless force.

He will believe and will lead us by faith to believe that Russia's objective of overcoming poverty and doing away with the struggle for existence is a good and valid objective for *us* and for the entire human race, and he will lead us to support that objective among the underdeveloped people of Africa, Asia, and South America, by the democratic methods that are dear to us.

These objectives will not be easy for us to pursue. They cannot succeed at all unless they are rooted in deep and relevant moral decisions. They will require us to answer all three of the great moral questions put before us by the God of our history with an unequivocal affirmative, in deliberate and thorough-going opposition to the answers given by Hitler. They will require us to return to the faith of our fathers in the world-wide unity of the human race, in the inherent and equal dignity and immeasurable possibilities in every human life, and in the possibility of a society upon this earth which will bring this unity of humanity into maturity, with ample opportunities for the development of individual culture for every human being and for those groups of human beings who are drawn together by precious spiritual ties.

These objectives will require the United States to accept and to discharge the responsibility of bringing the Western powers, of whom she is the leader, to a planned and programmed liquidation of the remnants of colonial power in Africa, Asia, and South America. They must give up once and for all the imperialistic habits of political domination, economic exploitation, and social humiliation of Asiatic, African, and South American peoples. These habits are themselves of the very essence of violence. They invite distrust and violence in return. It is not conceivable that the Western powers can win the confidence and goodwill of the peoples of Asia and Africa and South America as long as these habits persist in every so reduced an area.

These objectives will require the United States and the Western powers to accept the moral responsibility towards the whole of human life which goes with our enormous scientific, technical, organizational, and productive genius. They must prepare and execute a programme of economic reconstruction and aid on a world-wide basis, designed to overcome the animal-like struggle for existence which up to this time has prevailed over the earth, and to provide adequate food, clothing, housing, and health for every human family of every race, colour, nationality, and culture. The maximum progress possible towards these ends should be made within the generation now before us.

These objectives will require the United States, as the leader of this programme, to support it with whole-hearted and responsible adequacy, in an amount which may be equal to one-tenth or more of her annual productive power, and to elicit similar support from all her allies, persuading them to double and treble their available scientific and technical manpower.

These objectives will require that we set this programme before the world, not as an accessory to our military programme, but as the main objective, in relation to which our military programme is only a protective fence-building operation, and as evidence to the Russian people and their allies that, although we understandably fear their totalitarian organization and its related procedures of violence and subversion, we do believe in the sincerity and validity of their economic purposes, and that these purposes can be made not the enemy of political democracy, but the foundation of its success.

This is a plan on the highest level of statesmanship, designed to recognize and to encourage the Russian and Communist belief that a world-wide conquest of the struggle for existence is possible and to offer them a well-planned and significantly supported exhibition of working towards it by consultation and democratic co-operation on a universal basis. Such an example will strongly suggest an alternative to aggressive war, and to the violent and subversive establishment of totalitarian states, which we so greatly fear.

The plan involves a vast undertaking at huge and long-sustained cost. But this undertaking and this cost are within our power and are consistent with our honour. The plan is capable of preserving and enhancing the democratic countries' inheritance of free consultation, decision, and co-operation, and of giving them a world-wide power deeply rooted in the esteem and affection of all mankind. Whether we accept such objectives and such a programme is a matter of life or death for our civilization. The time is already very late.

5 / Legislating Human Rights in Ontario: I

LOUIS FINE

The Fair Employment Practices Act and the Fair Accommodation Practices Act are among the half dozen pieces of legislation, out of the hundreds in force in Ontario, which contain preambles describing their reason and intent. It has not been the fashion of the Legislature, in drafting and passing enactments, to make much use of the preamble. But in the case of the F.E.P. and F.A.P. laws, the Legislature departed from customary practice. To me, this is indicative that these laws hold a special position in the minds of our lawmakers.

The preamble to the Fair Employment Practices Act reads as follows: "Whereas it is contrary to public policy in Ontario to discriminate against men and women in respect of their employment because of race, creed, colour, nationality, ancestry or place of origin; whereas it is desirable to enact a measure designed to promote observance of this principle; and whereas to do so is in accord with the Universal Declaration of Human Rights as proclaimed by the United Nations; ..." The preamble to the Fair Accommodation Practices Act is couched in a similar vein. In my opinion, these declarations of public policy are among the most important parts of the two statutes. They affirm in unmistakable language that respect for the rights and dignity of every human being is a guiding principle of this Province. It is significant, too, that the preambles refer to the Universal Declaration of Human Rights, that great embodiment of the highest aspirations of mankind.

It is no idle boast to suggest that the Ontario Legislature has enacted a Human Rights Code which rivals the best of similar legislation in any other jurisdiction on this continent. Indeed, in many ways, the Province of Ontario has blazed the trail for this type of legislation in Canada. The development of the Code began in 1944 with the passage of the Racial Discrimination Act making it an offence to publish or display any notice, sign, symbol, or other representation expressing racial or religious discrimination. In 1950, the Labour Relations Act was amended to outlaw discrimination in collective agreements and, in the same year, discriminatory covenants in the sale of land were declared null and void. In 1951, the Fair Employment Practices Act was placed on the statute books and in 1954 the Fair Accommodation Practices Act became law.

Perhaps the most important piece of legislation in the whole Human Rights Code is the Act which established, in 1959, the Anti-Discrimination Commission and gave it the task of developing and conducting an educational programme throughout the province. This is a recognition of the fact that public enlightenment is one of the principal keys to a solution of the problem of discrimination.

From many years in Government service I have found that legislation does not remain static. It is dynamic, constantly responding to changing conditions and changing attitudes. Thus, in 1961, the Legislature saw fit to extend the coverage of the Fair Accommodation Practices Act into the realm of multiple housing accommodation and to change the name of our Commission. As time goes on, and as new needs become apparent, I have no doubt that our Human Rights Code will continue to keep pace with the requirements of the people of this Province. I believe that the Government and the Legislature will go on taking every step possible to see that discrimination is eliminated from our Province.

Of course, the mere existence of legislation on the statute books is far from being the total answer to any problem. This is particularly true with discrimination. We have excellent anti-discrimination legislation in Ontario, but, by itself, it cannot solve the problem of discrimination for it cannot wipe out acts of injustice. In baseball, hockey, or football, breaches of the rules take place despite the existence of rule books. If it were not for umpires and referees, mayhem would result. The officers of the Department of Labour, who are administering Ontario's fair practices laws and the members of the Human Rights Commission are, in a sense, umpires or referees in the delicate field of human relations, using the rules set forth in the Human Rights Code and endeavouring to prevent discrimination.

We who are involved in this field are firmly convinced of the value and the necessity of the legislation. We would be pretty poor souls, of course, if we did a job without believing in it, and a Commission that was composed of people who did not personally abhor the idea of discrimination would be a failure before it even started. We thus look upon our responsibility in this field as a sacred trust.

We recognize, of course, the power which prejudice holds, to a greater or a lesser degree, over all of us. Prejudice, the attitude of mind which gives rise to acts of discrimination, is rooted very deeply in human personality. It is based on lack of sensitivity, on misunderstanding, on ignorance, on wrongheadedness. At worst, it is the failure to recognize a fellow human being as a human being. Prejudice cannot be eliminated by the passage of a statute, but its outward manifestations can be curbed. Artificial barriers denying equality of opportunity to our fellow human beings can be breached and torn down. Nevertheless, great care must be exercised in the way in which the problem is approached. In combatting discrimination, we cannot afford to generate feelings of prejudice which would defeat our efforts. We have to be conscientious and understanding in our approach to people. We have no desire to force things down their throats, to persecute or to prosecute them.

What is the size and nature of the problem in Ontario? There is no doubt that prejudice exists in the minds of many people in this province and that it sometimes gives rise to acts of discrimination against individuals of particular races or creeds. We receive complaints each year, although not a great many, under both the Fair Employment Practices Act and the Fair Accommodation Practices Act. This is not to suggest that discrimination is at all widespread. Our experience is that virtually all of the complaints under the F.E.P. Act come from the major urban centres where relationships are generally much more impersonal. There is no clear pattern in these complaints. They arise in isolated cases and are not concentrated in any particular industry or group of industries. Several complaints come in each year under the F.A.P. Act against the resort industry and against such service industries as hotels and restaurants. We are most encouraged by the steps which the leaders of the resort industry are taking to promote a broader acceptance and practice of the law among their own membership. We have undertaken to help them in any way we can. Over the past few years, several cases of discrimination in the rental of apartment units have come to light. With the new legislation in this field, it is likely that there will be a number of complaints filed with the Department at first but undoubtedly these will taper off as knowledge of the law becomes more widespread.

There is a great deal of evidence that the situation in the realms of employment and accommodation has improved considerably over the past few years. We have seen firms open their doors to members of racial and religious groups who had previously been denied employment. We have seen those needless questions about racial origin and religion disappear from employment application forms. Coloured people who were formerly relegated to third-rate hotels and restaurants in Toronto can now obtain accommodation or meals wherever they desire to go.

Generally speaking, however, there is little information about the gravity of the discrimination problem in Ontario. This has made it difficult for the Commission to plan its programme. Fortunately, however, the School of Social Work at the University of Toronto has undertaken, under the very capable direction of Dr. Albert Rose, a study of the situation in the field of employment. This kind of study is something new in Canada and we hope that it will yield information which will not only be useful to those engaged in social work but will also help to make our own activities more effective.

The primary objective of our educational work has been to make the existence and the substance of the Human Rights Code as widely known as possible across the Province. Discrimination is a very different field from that covered by most other prohibitory statutes. We therefore cannot take it for granted that people know the law and will either obey it or be prosecuted for violating it. We do not want to prosecute but to prevent discrimination before it takes place. Prevention, rather than detection, is our basic principle. Indeed, we feel that the old rule about ignorance of the law being no excuse cannot be employed too strictly here; thus our job must be to make sure that such ignorance is kept to a minimum.

A number of privately sponsored organizations are doing excellent work in the realm of human rights. But in Canada at least, governmental participation in this area of education is relatively new and there is very little experience elsewhere upon which we can draw in planning educational activities. When there are no teachers, you have to train yourself; this is very much our position and our work has involved, therefore, a good deal of experimentation regarding the methods most suitable in this field.

We thought that the primary tool of our programme should be literature explaining the legislation and its enforcement. Accordingly, pamphlets and posters were prepared and we launched a quarterly bulletin. The next step was to get this material into circulation. Recognizing that our resources were not unlimited, we tried to direct the information to the places where it would do the most good—to the schools, churches, trade unions, community organizations of all kinds, to the leaders of opinion in all parts of Ontario, and to employers and purveyors of services and accommodation. In one year some 350,000 pieces of literature have been distributed across Ontario; our pamphlets have gone into every community. More than 10,000 individual letters were sent to clergymen of all denominations and faiths, mayors and reeves, newspaper editors, radio and TV proprietors, libraries, service clubs, fraternal societies, women's institutes, labour unions, and so forth. In each case, lines of co-operation were suggested for assisting our work and proposals were invited for improving it. Clergymen and persons associated with community and other organizations undertook to make our basic pamphlets available to their people. Newspapers and radio and TV stations publicized the Human Rights Code. A number of libraries arranged special book displays and circulated reading lists on the subject of human rights. A large number of municipal councils officially endorsed the aims of the Code and drew to the attention of their communities the rights and duties embodied in it. The net result was that we made contacts with several thousand people in all parts of Ontario. The response to these efforts, far greater than we had dared to expect, was most gratifying. It indicated that there is a great body of opinion in Ontario ready and willing to take up and work for the cause of human rights.

December 10, 1960, was the twelfth anniversary of the Universal Declaration of Human Rights and we felt that it was a fitting occasion to make special efforts to acquaint the people of Ontario with their own Human Rights Code. The then Premier, Mr. Frost, whose deep concern for this cause is well known, and whose understanding and support helped us so greatly in our formative period, in a public statement called upon the people of Ontario to find an occasion during the week of December 4 to re-study the principles of that great Declaration and to re-examine the state of human rights practices.

We sought to provide material which would be useful to clergymen and the leaders of church groups, to students and teachers, and to community organizations in planning programmes around the theme of human rights during that period. The Minister of Education asked all the secondary schools in the province to observe the week of December 4 as Human Rights Week and, in co-operation with his department, special activities for the week's programme, together with special discussion material, including books and plays, were suggested to the schools. Radio and television were most co-operative and generous with their time. They brought the Human Rights Code to the attention of their listeners and viewers through spot announcements, panel discussions, and special programmes. Every radio station in Ontario broadcast as a public service a short talk on human rights by the then Minister of Labour, the Honourable Charles Daley, to whom this Commission reported. All of these served to make the people of Ontario more familiar with the existence and substance of the law and were in line with what we assume should be the first objective of an educational programme.

Having won support from the schools of Ontario, we hope to reach and win the minds and hearts of youngsters across Ontario. It is, of course, true that prejudice is not an inherent characteristic of human beings, but an acquired outlook.

Little children do not discriminate. They learn from the example of their elders. It is only in their later school years that they begin to absorb and act on the biases of adult society. If steps can be taken to prevent the development of prejudice in the early years of schooling, much of the problem of discrimination will be solved. We hope to enlist the help of school authorities and teachers throughout Ontario in developing means of reaching the younger generation.

We have reached the stage where, on paper at least, we have made a great many useful contacts across the province. But we recognize that the administration of certain statutes and the operation of a publicity campaign constitute only a framework of achievement. These things, by themselves, would fall far short of guaranteeing across Ontario the desired attitudes of respect for the dignity and rights of every human being. A full structure is required. Individuals must be encouraged to think for themselves about the great issues of human rights and to participate directly in the promotion of enlightenment and understanding in their own communities.

We intend to broaden our efforts to achieve these ends. Our budget has been increased substantially by the Legislature. We are continuing to distribute literature and to publish our bulletin, *Human Relations*. The purpose of the bulletin is to help stimulate thought, to broaden the public's understanding of the cause of human rights, and to win acceptance of the principles of the Human Rights Code.

We are considering a number of additional approaches. One is to make greater use of radio and television. Another is to encourage the showing of films on human rights; a number of good films are available in film libraries across Ontario. We would like to see a greater use made of plays and books on the subject which are currently available. We hope to stimulate further study and discussion at all levels of the educational system and in organizations of all kinds throughout Ontario.

We have taken some steps to meet employers and purveyors of accommodation and services in order to discuss with them the meaning and nature of their responsibilities under the human rights legislation. We hope to broaden this activity in the coming year.

In my view, the vast majority of employers and of persons who provide accommodation or services are conscientiously striving to observe the law. There are a few, however, who do persist in thinking with their pocketbooks, rather than with their minds and hearts. They support a no-discrimination policy in principle but they are afraid to apply it consistently. They believe—quite mistakenly—that the granting to people of certain racial or religious backgrounds the common, ordinary rights which they accord automatically and as a matter of course to everybody else, will cause trouble for them and will lose them business. Experience indicates that such fears are totally without foundation. There are also people who suffer from amnesia on this question of human rights, forgetting that they were at one time themselves members of minority groups which suffered from discrimination. Today, they discriminate against somebody else.

We all agree that respect for the dignity and the rights of every human being is the foundation stone of peace and justice in this country and this world. The promotion of the kind of society where men and women of all races and creeds can come together in co-operation and goodwill is the basic objective of Ontario's programme for human rights.

6 / Legislating Human Rights in Ontario: II

THOMAS M. EBERLEE

The cause of human rights is so important to our province, our nation and, indeed, to the whole world, that it merits being approached with missionary fervour. In Canada today, the principle of human rights is widely accepted and practised. But such has not always been the case, as many well know. Indeed, the pages of our history are all too frequently besmirched by a sad record of conflicts and acts of injustice with a racial or a religious basis.

Canada's history began in an atmosphere of strife between different racial and religious backgrounds. Very early in our development we relegated the Indian to the limbo of our national life. When desperate people escaped the inequality of their homelands and came to this great half-continent, they discovered too often that the New World was new only in the geographical sense. Racial and religious feuds of other lands had been merely transferred to a new locale and they found expression in exclusiveness, in discrimination, and even in open conflict. They were reflected in barriers to employment, in signs that read, "No Irishmen need apply," or "No Englishmen need apply," in facilities that were for "Gentiles Only," and so forth.

Fortunately for Canada, as the ink has dried on pages of injustice, new chapters reflecting the conscience and the practical good sense of our people have been written. Canadians have gradually subordinated their differences in a common striving towards the construction of a great nation. This is manifest in many milestones along the path of our history: Baldwin and Lafontaine, with their different backgrounds, coming together more than one hundred years ago to operate a new experiment in self-government; Macdonald and Cartier, and their associates of both English- and French-speaking origin, uniting half a dozen separate and widely separated colonies into a great Confederation and changing their vision of a transcontinental nation into concrete reality. Our history is studded with similar evidence of a growth of mutual understanding, co-operation, and goodwill between men and women of every race, colour, and creed and of the remarkable achievements which the operation of this policy has wrought for our nation. Ontario's Human Rights Code not only stems from these developments but is also calculated to strengthen this policy by guaranteeing to every person certain basic rights, regardless of race, colour, or creed.

In 1944, we were fighting to preserve Canada's freedom. There was at that time a realization that discrimination and inequality within our own borders were just as serious threats to that freedom as the might of the enemy. Moreover, we had before us the fearful and tragic example of the destructive power of racism, as practised in the gas chambers of the Third Reich. It was in this context that the Ontario Legislature enacted its first human rights statute—the Racial Discrimination Act. This law prohibited the publishing or displaying of any notice, sign, symbol, or other representation expressing racial or religious discrimination. The Racial Discrimination Act now forms part of the Fair Accommodation Practices Act.

The year 1950 saw the passage of two new anti-discrimination laws, a section of the Labour Relations Act which nullifies any collective agreement that discriminates against any person on racial or religious grounds, and a section of the Conveyancing and Law of Property Act which renders null and void any discriminatory covenant in the sale of land.

A year later, Ontario became the first Canadian jurisdiction to enact a Fair Employment Practices Act. I was a university student then and just by chance happened to sit in the gallery of the Legislature one night when the bill was being debated. In the interests of passing exams, the mind of a university student is often more taken up with and aware of the trends of thought in the period of the Peloponnesian Wars than with current social developments. At least, that was the case with me ten years ago. I remember being surprised at the legislation and very much impressed with its spirit. I did not know that similar legislation had been enacted two or three years earlier in New York State and that it certainly had proven effective in opening the doors of employment to minority groups. My reaction was that the bill was fine but it probably wouldn't work.

I believe my view was shared by a large number of people. Many were apprehensive that the Act would not be acceptable, but their worries were soon quieted. Of course, no law will work if people do not believe in it. Obviously this was the situation on this continent with such laws as those prohibiting the manufacture and use of alcoholic beverages. In the case of the Fair Employment Practices Act, it became apparent that the law was completely in line with the thinking of the vast majority of the population and that the people of Ontario were going to make it work. The provisions of the Act itself, with its emphasis upon conciliation and persuasion in the settlement of cases, have served both to make it effective and to win for it wide public acceptance.

The principal prohibitory clause of the Act reads as follows: "No employer or person acting on behalf of an employer shall refuse to employ or to continue to employ any person or discriminate against any person in regard to employment or any term or condition of employment because of his race, creed, colour, nationality, ancestry or place of origin." Thus, the law provides sanctions against discrimination not only in the initial selection of an employee, but also in the treatment of an employee on the job, including dismissal. The Act also makes it unlawful for a trade union to exclude from membership or expel or suspend any person because of race, creed, colour, etc. It prohibits the use of job application forms or the publication of any employment advertisement, or the making of any written or oral inquiry which expresses any limitation, specification, or preference as to the race, creed, or colour of any person.

The Department of Labour receives an average of 20 to 25 complaints a year under the Act. Many of them allege discrimination in connection with a refusal of employment. A large number of them deal with questions on application forms—such needless queries as religion, place of birth, and so forth. So far as I know, there has been only one complaint against a trade union in the past decade and that involved a proposed change in the constitution of a particular union requiring its members to be Canadian citizens. Of course, the labour movement in this country has, for many years, been one of the strongest proponents of anti-discrimination legislation and its excellent standing, as far as our own complaint records are concerned, is a reflection of this attitude and of the strong educational campaign operated under the sponsorship of the Ontario Labour Committee for Human Rights. Over the years, there have been virtually no complaints about alleged discrimination in connection with "any term or condition of employment." Conceivably, these words would permit action to be taken if a person were demoted or refused a promotion on grounds of race, colour, or creed. But I do not think an occasion has yet arisen for them to be tested.

Certain types of employers and employment are exempted from the provisions of the Act. It does not apply to exclusively religious, philanthropic, educational, fraternal or social organizations not operated for private profit or to any organization that is operated primarily to foster the welfare of a religious or ethnic group. Nor does it apply in such essentially personal situations as domestic employment in private homes or commercial establishments with fewer than five employees. While one can only deplore the practice of discrimination within these categories, it seems to me that they do fall outside the area of public policy and therefore it is reasonable that they should be exempted. Yet, it is our impression that many employers in this "exempt area" do adhere voluntarily to the terms of the Act on grounds of good citizenship and exemplary conduct.

What happens when a complaint is received by the Department of Labour? A conciliation officer is appointed immediately to look into the case. He talks to the complainant and obtains his statement of the facts. He then discusses the matter with the party against whom the complaint has been lodged. If necessary, he calls both parties in for a face-to-face session on the complaint. In every case handled in the past decade, the mediation afforded by these steps has sufficed to bring about a settlement of the difficulty. In only a few cases is deliberate discrimination revealed as a policy of an employer. More often the trouble has been caused by a misunderstanding, based on extreme sensitivity, or by a minor official, who, in denying employment to an individual on grounds of race or creed, does not realize that this is contrary to the policy of the management of the company. Unfortunately, there are cases where an individual's lack of educational or other qualifications, rather than his race or creed, is really the cause of his failure to obtain the job. It is often difficult for people to accept this as the real reason.

Should a conciliation officer be unable to bring the parties into a position of understanding and agreement, the Fair Employment Practices Act provides further settlement procedures, but, as indicated, it has never been necessary to use them. As a next step, the Minister of Labour has the power to appoint a board, similar in function to a conciliation board in a labour dispute, which would hear evidence from all the parties involved and make recommendations for settling the matter. The Minister has the power to make whatever order he deems necessary to carry out the recommendations of the board and his order is final and binding. Finally, the Act provides penalties by way of summary conviction for any person who fails to comply with the Act or with any order made under it. It has, of course, never yet been necessary to prosecute.

It is difficult to gauge accurately the effect which the Fair Employment Practices Act has had on broadening equality of opportunity in employment, but we feel that it has been substantial. We know of many firms which have opened their doors over the past ten years to persons from previously excluded minority groups. We know that discriminatory questions have largely disappeared from application forms in Ontario. One never sees employment advertisements in the press these days which indicate any limitations of a racial or religious nature. In fact, the press has been most co-operative in stopping the publication of such ads. Many times in the course of a year, the Fair Employment Practices Branch receives enquiries from newspapers about the propriety of certain wordings for advertisements. Without exception, where the branch has expressed doubts about the advertisement in question, the wording has been changed to comply with the law.

One other interesting piece of evidence of the beneficial effect of the F.E.P. Act came to light last summer in an experiment reported by Mr. Pierre Berton in the Toronto

Star. In 1950, a girl with a so-called "Jewish-sounding" name was able to make appointments for an interview for a job with only 17 out of 47 employers who had advertised for help, while a girl with a "Gentile-sounding" name secured interviews with 41 of the 47. By 1960, Mr. Berton reported, the situation had so improved that the girl with the "Jewish name" was granted interviews by 40 out of 48 prospective employers and her Gentile counterpart by only one more. To Mr. Berton, this was indicative of "true progress."

I should like to turn now to the Fair Accommodation Practices Act which was placed on the statute books in 1954. Its principal clause provided that "no person shall deny to any person or class of persons the accommodation, services or facilities available in any place to which the public is customarily admitted because of the race, creed, colour, nationality, ancestry or place of origin of such person or class of persons." A further clause has been added to the Act which extends the right of equality of access beyond public facilities and into the area of multiple housing. The Legislature, at the Session which ended in the spring of 1961, has made it unlawful to discriminate in respect to the renting or occupancy of self-contained apartment units in buildings containing more than six units. This is a notable advance. Ontario was the first province in Canada to legislate in the fields of both employment and accommodation and now it is blazing the trail in multiple housing. Only a handful of jurisdictions on the continent have gone this far in upholding the rights of their citizens. Public reaction to this development in the growth of our Human Rights Code suggests that it, too, is completely in line with our people's traditional concept of justice and concern for the dignity of every human being.

The procedures for the settlement of complaints under the F.A.P. Act are precisely the same as those adopted for the Fair Employment Practices Act. The F.A.P. Act has, admittedly, presented a larger number of problems than the Fair Employment Practices Act. Because the setting is more personal, prejudice is more often translated into acts of discrimination in the area of accommodation and services than in that of employment. Many of the complaints reaching the Department of Labour concern such establishments as tourist resorts; others are connected with service in restaurants and hotels. Invariably, however, the response to the Department's efforts at settlement is co-operative and constructive. Only two complaints have led to prosecutions under this Act. The new section on multiple housing will soon be in effect. Meanwhile the necessary administrative machinery is being made ready. Already enquiries have been received and a fair number of complaints are anticipated, at least within the first few months of operation. This is not to suggest, of course, that the number will be large—perhaps on the order of fifteen or twenty in the first year.

Over the years, legislative sanctions and educational programmes have been employed by themselves in efforts to promote the kind of society in which respect for human dignity and a belief in equality of opportunity hold sway. Experience suggests that a complete reliance on legal sanctions or, alternatively, educational efforts, does not produce the optimum results. For that reason, we believe that law and enlightenment must be employed together. The one supports and strengthens the other.

Our name has just been changed to Human Rights Commission, and we are the only Human Rights Commission operated by a Government anywhere in the world. It may be asked: "What's in a name?" We feel there is a good deal in our change of name and we are proud to be associated with this re-designated body. Our new name is positive; we stand *for* human rights rather than merely *against* discrimination. We feel that our work will meet with a much greater measure of public support and co-operation if our name indicates a positive approach. Our new name gives a clearer picture of our purpose: the Commission was conceived as a shield for the dignity and rights of *every* person in Ontario. After all, the cause of human rights does not concern a few individuals or a few groups in our Provincial community who may be victimized by discrimination. It concerns everybody, for we are all victimized when acts of injustice occur. Not only is our sense of fair play insulted, but those basic principles which are essential to decent human society are contradicted and overturned. The very foundations of our freedom are threatened.

There are few issues in our world today as real, as big, or as pressing as the question of civilized relationships between individuals and groups of varying racial or religious backgrounds. We see policies being pursued and events occurring elsewhere in the world that present frightening possibilities for conflict and bloodshed. And yet we also see trends developing in the midst of frustration and humiliation that give promise of a better day. As for ourselves, we cannot be complacent about the state of human rights practices here. Not, for example, when a young doctor comes from Ghana to study in our land of freedom and justice and is turned away from two apartment houses in this city because, in the stark language of discrimination, "We don't rent to Negroes."

From a basically English-French-speaking partnership, our population has expanded to include men and women from every quarter of the globe. In the years ahead, we can expect to welcome even greater numbers from other lands who will bring with them their own cultural and religious traditions, their own skills and creative talents. Our lives and theirs will be the richer, and Canada's progress will be the greater, if they are made to feel that they have come not to a melting pot where they must subordinate their individuality but to a nation whose development has always been based on the harmonious integration of its component parts.

Here is a cause that is worth fighting for. But it needs strong support from the leaders of Ontario; men and women who can preach it and teach it. Human rights are dependent in no small measure on the attitude of the individual citizen and his sense of obligation to his fellow men. Of course, we have structures of legal and educational activity, but these are merely the bare bones of the programme. To give them flesh and blood and life, people all over Ontario must become interested and involved in forwarding these principles—because the fact remains that human rights are in everybody's hands.

Part Three: Government

ANDREW STEWART

PAUL H. DOUGLAS

JOHN C. BENNETT

PAUL H. DOUGLAS

7 / Communicating the Truth: Ethical Dilemmas of Radio and Television

ANDREW STEWART

In this paper I shall confine my attention to radio and especially television, that is, to the broadcast media. I cannot pretend to have any familiarity with the press as a medium of communication. There are, I know, certain differences between the press and broadcasting which are not unrelated to the problem of truth in communication. Certainly we treat the two media differently. In the newspaper, matter competes for space; on the broadcasting station it competes for time. However, the scarcity of space in newspapers is not absolute as the scarcity of time can be in broadcasting; and this is not unimportant to the problem of selection. The editorial page can become two pages without reducing the space available for the comics, and another page of advertising can be added without reducing the space available for news. On the other hand, once a broadcasting station is in full operation each minute taken for advertising is withdrawn from some other purpose; an increase in the time allowed for discussion of current affairs means a reduction in the time for entertainment. The newspaper can be set aside and picked up again. But there is an immediacy about the television message; the image on the set is fleeting and cannot be recovered or returned to. The watching of television is usually a shared experience, but the newspaper is read individually. The pages can be separated out so that father is reading the comics, and mother the society page, while junior is scanning the news columns to complete his school assignment on "The Activities of the U.N. in the Congo" (the editorial page is on the floor). These and other differences between the press and broadcasting are all significant. Further, society acts differently towards the two media. In principle, and under law, anyone may start up his own printing press if he wishes to do so; broadcasting stations are licensed to broadcast exclusively on particular channels, and the number of available channels is limited. Broadcasting stations operate under legislation by which they are made subject to regulations. No similar legislation and regulations apply to newspapers. But these significant differences notwithstanding, I suspect that many of the things that can be said about the ethics of broadcasting apply equally to the press.

The invention of language enabled man to draw upon the experiences of the past, both his own and those of others; to extend his thoughts into the future, and thus to influence the future of himself and others; to describe the relations he observed between himself and his environment and the motions which take place in nature; and to engage in speculation about "how" and "why." The history of communication is the record of a continuous extension of man's capacity to transfer ideas over time and space. Early man found it possible to give permanence to the expression of his ideas by painting or carving on the walls of caves; and the development of writing, the alphabet, and the printed word further extended the boundaries of time. The limitations of distance were overcome by drum and smoke signals and by means of the horse and boat. Given the means of recording ideas, the speed and range of communication was extended by developments in transportation—the steamship, locomotive, automobile, and aeroplane. The telegraph was the first invention permitting almost immediate communication over long distances. It was followed by the telephone, wireless telegraphy, radio, and television. Without complicating the matter by referring to the technical aspects, the legal definition of broadcasting, which includes radio and television, describes it as the dissemination of signals which are intended to be received by the public. The signals are released into space in such a manner that they can be picked up by anyone who has the necessary receiving equipment; hence, radio and television are referred to as mass media of communication.

The developments in communication have expanded immeasurably the horizons of man's thought and have given him a wealth of vicarious experiences. Whatever the problems of adjustment may be we must believe that successful adjustment will add to his stature. But the adjustments are difficult. Today communication ranges from the simple, direct conversation between two people to the complex industry of television in which specialists engage in the production of vehicles for the transmission of ideas—films, tapes, and rehearsed programmes; other specialists select and assemble the vehicles and broadcast the messages they contain; and large numbers of persons receive the messages as spectators, listeners, or consumers. The whole process is complicated, obscure, indirect, and impersonal.

Who is it in this sprawling network of activities that is the conveyor of ideas? The licensees who own broadcasting transmission facilities are referred to as the "broadcasters," but to a considerable extent they act only as middlemen bringing together programmes produced in a variety of places and by many people all of whom have some part in the determination of the communication that takes place. Even within the organization of the broadcasting company, making decisions is a diffused and complex process. In Canada the usual situation is a privately owned broadcasting station carrying some programmes supplied by the publicly owned Canadian Broadcasting Corporation. The C.B.C. is maintained in large part by public funds supplied to it by Parliament. Its powers and duties are set out in the Broadcasting Act, and could be changed at any time by the expressed wish of Parliament. The Corporation has its Board of Directors, Executive Officers, and management staff. Within this structure decisions are worked out which result in the broadcasting of programmes with given content. But the programmes available depend on the participation of many others. The Corporation has contracts with news gathering services for the supply of news; with directors who select and edit programme "continuity"; with producers who determine the manner in which programmes are presented; with organized suppliers and producers of programmes. In its own productions the Corporation must rely on creative artists and individual performers. All these people influence the ideas which are expressed on television during the hours reserved for programmes of the C.B.C. Within the private company which operates a station there is the same diffusion of decision-making. Because the station operator relies wholly on advertising revenues to support his operations during the time not set aside for programmes of the Corporation, his decisions are considerably influenced by the participation of the advertisers. In this complex situation, who is the conveyor of ideas, corresponding to the speaker who addresses an audience? He is not one but many people.

The audience consists of those people who are watching television at any one time. The size of the audience can roughly be determined. Where there is a choice of programmes, for example in an area served by two stations, if more people are tuned in to Station A than to Station B we conclude that more people prefer the programme on A than the one on B. If the difference is of some magnitude this is probably a correct deduction. The combination of programmes on the two stations, at any time period, which will attract the largest audience is a reflection of majority preferences. However, when the members of the audience do not have a chance to register their preferences by offering to give up something in exchange (i.e., to pay for service) the outcome is not affected by the intensity of the preferences. If there were no differences in ability to pay and each set owner could bid for programmes of different types, the results in terms of programmes shown might be substantially different. Nevertheless, the solution is always a matter of choice. When this paper was delivered, members of the audience were there for various reasons; but whatever they were they had chosen to come to listen to a speaker on a particular topic. There were, however, many other people who chose to stay away and to do other things, including watching television. It is likely that some of my audience (I hope not too many) wished they had stayed at home beside the set. It might have comforted them to know that a substantial proportion of those at home watching television were not enjoying what they were seeing. Actually it would have been easier for them to turn off the set than for any of my audience to rise and leave; but most of them probably stayed with it, presumably because they did not know what else to do.

A great many people take part in communication by television, both as conveyors and receivers of ideas; all of them have some influence on the nature of the communication. It may be that the effectiveness of the individual participant differs; but there should be no difference in the obligation that rests on each of them to seek to preserve the integrity of communication. Each of those engaged in the production of the vehicles of communication should make the effort to be honest with himself in the formulation and expression of his ideas; and each assembler in the selection he makes. It is said that under conditions of free enterprise the consumers of the products of the television industry get what they want. Does this mean that if, in the honest judgment of the broadcaster, what the audience wants is to have their fears and prejudices fed, those engaged in the broadcasting industry, having no mind, conscience, or obligation to themselves, should lend their efforts to these ends? It is hard to believe that it should be so. Each member of the audience should make the effort to be honest with himself in his attitude to and perception of the ideas communicated to him. If, in the judgment of any member of the audience, he is receiving either the biased views of those engaged in the industry, in whatever capacity, or the fears and prejudices of others, having a mind, conscience, and obligation to himself, he should make a protest by his actions and his voice. He should, however, first make his best effort to ensure that what he is advancing are not merely his own biased views, fears, and prejudices.

Advertising has become inextricably involved with broadcasting. The use of broadcasting for communicating advertising messages is a legitimate and effective one. Advertising, of course, is not confined to broadcasting, and this is not the place to attempt a full discussion of the ethics of advertising. At the risk of distortion by simplification, let me try to set out the ethical dilemma as I see it. I have noticed recently two advertisements placed by the Association of Canadian Advertisers in the public transport vehicles of Ottawa. The advertisements claim that without advertising many goods and services now enjoyed by consumers would not have been made available, and that without advertising consumers would not reap the benefit of mass production and lower prices. This is merely to say that advertising contributes to an increase in the material standards of life. The advertisements are presumably placed by the Association in order to create public attention favourable to the advertisers and I am sure advertisers honestly believe that their advertising contributes to the public good. In a general sense, so do I. The statements of relations in the advertisements are, in my opinion, valid generalizations that can be tested and substantiated by observation and analysis.

The achievement of a high material standard of living is, of course, an indirect effect of the performance of the advertising function. The immediate purpose is to sell goods and services by inducing consumers to buy. If consumers can be induced to purchase on the basis of representations and claims which depart from the truth, new products can be established and techniques of mass production employed, and by these tests the process can be said to advance the public good. This is the dilemma of means and ends.

Recently, in another country, the nation was shocked by the exposure of flagrant deception perpetrated over a period of time on a television programme. After the discovery, a young man who participated in the fraud was reported as having said that although "deeply troubled by the deceit" he was making "more money than I ever dreamed of having," and he added "I was almost able to convince myself that it did not matter what I was doing because it was having such a good effect on the national attitude towards teachers, education and intellectual life." This is the kind of rationalization and self-deception to which we are led by permitting ends to justify means. Does the end result of increased consumption of goods and services justify means which involve departure from the truth? What does it profit a society to maintain a high and expanding standard of living on a structure which is not based on the truth? The dilemma confronts the advertiser: Is it more important to promote sales than to preserve truth? Is the pursuit of truth in the advertising message more important than its sales impact? The dilemma confronts the buyer: How important is it to make the effort to discover the truth and to follow its dictates? In a recent article I came across the following: "The ideal statement should be formulated 'A given piece of advertising should make the product look different from other products, *without violating the truth.*'" Why "without violating the truth"? The concept that what is not false is true is surely the lowest possible criterion of truth. It suggests that what we are confronted with is a simple choice between "the true" and "the false." The problem is more difficult than this. Merely to seek to avoid violating the truth is a negative approach. The ethical approach is to make a conscientious effort to press towards the truth.

The Canadian Association of Broadcasters was engaged for some time in devising a "Broadcasting Code of Ethics"; that Code was published in February 1961. The principle of self-regulation of the industry by a Code of Ethics which declares the ethical responsibilities of the broadcaster is a sound one. The exercise of preparing it requires broadcasters to give thought and expression to their purposes; the publication of the Code is an act of communication which presents the opportunity for participation by others, and it is a commitment to act accordingly. The clause dealing with "News" is especially relevant. The statement is an excellent one, as far as it goes—by which I mean only that it is impossible to be complete in a statement of two or three hundred words. The Clause distinguishes between news and editorial comment, and suggests that on the air each should be clearly labelled for what it is. "Nothing in the foregoing shall be understood as preventing news broadcasters from analyzing and elucidating news so long as such analysis or comment is clearly labelled as such and kept distinct from regular news presentations. Member stations will, insofar as practical, endeavour to provide editorial opinion which shall be clearly labelled as such and kept entirely distinct from regular broadcasts of news or analysis and opinion." The distinction here made is important; and the listener should be clear whether the words he hears fall into one category or the other.

"The fundamental purpose of news dissemination in a democracy is to enable people to know what is happening, and to understand events so that they may form their own conclusions.... It shall be the responsibility of member stations to ensure that news shall be presented with accuracy and without bias. The member station shall satisfy itself that the arrangements made for obtaining news ensure this result." Broadcasting stations usually have their own news room staff who engage in the gathering of, mainly, local news; they also have arrangements with news services so that information on national and international events is coming in on the wires continuously. The purpose of the news room is to "enable people to know what is happening." But it is impossible to give them the whole record of what is happening on the local, national, and international scene. It is necessary in the process of compiling the news bulletins to select and reduce. How can we be sure that the condensation of events is a true record of what is happening? The answer obviously is that we cannot. We are dependent on those who make the selections for us. Although it is possible to find means of checking on local news, we still are almost completely at the mercy of others when it comes to knowing what is happening in, say, Algiers. The ultimate protection we have is that these others are earnestly and conscientiously trying to prepare a true record for us; that they value the truth beyond anything else.

I recall living in a town which had two daily newspapers. The editorial pages were both highly partisan in politics, and it was difficult to believe that news accounts of political meetings referred to the same event. Such an experience, and it is a common one, cannot help but throw doubt upon the veracity of the operation and the integrity of those providing the news.

Other ethical dilemmas confront the news department of a paper or a broadcasting station. Again, I take an example from personal experience. Universities have their tragedies; and when I served as president of a university, I once, with some hesitation, called the editor of a newspaper asking him to withhold the name of a student who had committed suicide. The decision must rest on the mind and conscience of the newsman. Public figures, by reason of their position, are news, and perhaps they have no claim to privacy; but surely the person who lives quietly and unobtrusively is entitled to some reticence in the disclosure of the manner of his dying. There is much that is happening that is ugly and sordid. The newsman must record these things; but if he is honest he will not allow his own interest in such matters to influence the weight given to them in describing the totality of events. Does a murder or sex crime, with all its lurid details, really rate top priority in a newscast of what is happening at any time in the city of Toronto? If the answer is that this is the kind of news people want, one must again ask the question whether the newsman is not being dishonest with himself—is he honestly trying to tell people what is happening, or is he trying to feed people what they want to hear?

Publishers, including broadcasting stations, are continuously being provided with information which someone wants them to release. I am not referring to the large volume of public service announcements which are carried by stations without charge, in the interests of community activities, welfare organizations, and the like (although sometimes even these can create problems). Usually in the latter type of announcement the sources are quite clearly designated. But information is fed to the media of communications by organizations, or their agents, in the hope and with the expectation that its publication will influence people. Such information is variously referred to as the issue of press releases, public relations, or propaganda. Whether the objects may be judged "good" or "bad," the process creates a problem for the honest newsman.

When we come to the consideration of editorializing we are in the realm of opinion. On most matters of importance there is room for honest differences of opinion, and differences of opinion will exist. Editorializing thus involves controversial broadcasting.

The principles governing controversial broadcasting are set out in a document published by the Board of Broadcast Governors. The document says, in part:

> Non-commercial organizations or societies interested in public affairs may purchase time on subsidiary hookups or individual stations.... Each broadcast must be preceded and concluded by appropriate announcements making clear the nature and substance of the broadcast, and indicating that equal facilities are available on the same basis for the expression of opposing views....
> In accordance with its policy of resisting any attempts to regiment opinion or to abuse freedom of speech, the Board lays down no specific rulings covering controversial broadcasting. The Board itself supports the policy of the fullest use of the air for: (a) forthright discussion of all controversial questions; (b) equal and fair presentation of all main points of view; (c) the discussion of current affairs and problems by informed, authoritative and competent speakers. Broadcasting is a changing and evolving art and no fixed and permanent criteria can be set down for the best method of presenting controversial material. These policies have been adopted in an effort to ensure that the medium of broadcasting may remain at the disposal of the nation, regardless of party, section, class or creed.

The principle of freedom of speech, and the correlative principles of "equal access" and "the right to reply," are fundamental in the matter of controversial broadcasting. To these should be added "information with respect to sources." In defending this latter principle Mr. Justice Hugo Black, in the United States, did so on the grounds that it, in turn, rested on the "fundamental constitutional principle that our people adequately informed may be able to distinguish between the true and the false." I am not sure that the assumption is always valid, or that the problem is as simple as that of a choice between "the true" and "the false"; and yet it rests on the basic belief in the integrity of man and on respect for his personality. "Our people" are entitled to know whose opinions are being presented to them and who it is that seeks to capture their minds. The principle of freedom of speech and of communication of opinions honestly held can also be defended on the grounds that it is a means towards the discovery of the truth. If truth as we perceive it is never tested against the truth as others see it, it cannot be further illuminated except by our own experiences. But the willingness to test our perception in this way depends upon a tolerance for the perceptions of others. We ought not, of course, to tolerate dishonesty; and the root of the problem of communication remains that of honesty and integrity in those who participate.

Two things are clear. We cannot expect "the truth"; indeed we are probably incapable of recognizing it. It is a dangerous assumption that any one person or group of persons is custodian of "the truth." We can, then, only expect to approach truth through communication to the extent that everyone participating in communication sets a high value on the search for truth. How do we seem to perform, in these terms, in the mass media of communication? The only possible answer is, not well enough. I suspect this answer would meet with universal assent; and this is a good sign because it implies that the search for truth goes on.

At the same time there are some things which it is prudent for us to do. First, we should mark out certain points of responsibility. I have referred to the fact that the material to be communicated passes through the minds of many people; and that decision-making is widely diffused. This is a good thing; but it is well to define certain points at which a special measure of responsibility must be taken. Under the Broadcasting Act, the licensed broadcasters—networks and stations —are held legally responsible; and as those immediately related in the chain of communication with the receiving public, this is reasonable. "In the long run, the responsibility for keeping the communication channels open and working properly must be borne primarily by those engaged in the business of communication. It is up to those who control the spotlight of publicity to see that it is bright enough and properly focussed." Second, we should ensure that the channels of communication do not fall under the control of a small number of people, or that the material of communication is derived from a limited number of sources, no matter what economies might be effected thereby. To quote again from the Board's document on controversial broadcasting: "The air belongs to the people, who are entitled to hear the principal points of view on all questions of importance. The air must not fall under the control of any individual or group influenced by reason of their wealth or special position." Third, we must insist on the fullest possible disclosure of what goes on in the areas of communication. Broadcasting is itself news, and should be dealt with on the general principles that govern news dissemination. This applies to the activities of the Board of Broadcast Governors as much as to other parts of the broadcasting system. The obligation to pursue truth, which I have contended rests upon those engaged in broadcasting, rests equally on the Board in the performance of its functions. I have set out my views on this in an address entitled "The Administrator as Judge," in which I state:

The pursuit of a conclusion requires a disciplined application of the mind. There must be a conscious effort to determine what is relevant and to exclude the irrelevant; to appraise the significance of cause and effect relations; to weigh the balance of considerations in each case.... The process cannot be accurately described, but the willingness and capacity of the administrator to pursue it is essential. It can, perhaps, best be described as the passion for intellectual integrity; the recognition of a problem, the acceptance of a mental challenge to come to grips with it, the capacity to derive satisfaction from engaging in the process, a distaste for anything less than the maximum effort, an unwillingness to fool oneself.

Finally, we need an alert public. The broadcasting system— broadcasting stations, the Canadian Broadcasting Corporation, the Board of Broadcast Governors—operates under legislation passed by the Parliament of Canada. There is an obligation on Parliament and on its instruments of enquiry to seek for truth in its relation to broadcast communications. Broadcasters, the Board, and Parliament are people; they are not much different, if at all, from the general public. Perhaps because of the special positions they hold they may be expected to offer some leadership; but they will also tend to reflect the attitudes of the society of which they are a part. Consequently we need a public alert to examine their own attitudes as well as the attitudes of those they hold responsible.

The pursuit of truth in communication is not easy. It takes effort and the will to make the effort. This raises another problem: the development of the will to seek truth. It is surely not wrong to assume that religion should contribute to this need. You are familiar with the words of Solomon, Son of David, King of Israel: "Yes, if thou criest after Knowledge and liftest up thy voice for understanding; if thou seekest her as silver and searchest for her as high treasures; then shalt thou understand the fear of the Lord and find the Knowledge of God." The University with which I was associated for many years has as its motto "Quaecumque Vera" meaning "Whatsoever things are true." The words are part of the injunction of Paul in his letter to the Philippians: "Finally, brethren, whatsoever things are true, whatsoever things are honest, whatsoever things are lovely, whatsoever things are of good report; if there be any virtue and if there be any praise, think on these things." But the question recorded as having been put by Pilate, the Roman Governor, to the Young Rabbi from Nazareth "What is truth?" remains unanswered.

What is important is the pursuit of truth, the value that is attached to the quest for truth. If you ask me why the search for truth is important, I can only answer that truth is "what lies at the heart of things," and, in the words of Solomon, if we value truth sufficiently and seek it diligently we move towards the "Knowledge of God."

8 / Ethical Problems in Politics

PAUL H. DOUGLAS

The central problem of all democratic governments, one that is particularly acute in a large country, is the problem of governing in the general interest, in the interest of the people as a whole rather than in the interest of specific groups.

Plato, after watching Athenian democracy operate for many years, and having seen it go through the Peloponnesian wars and put Socrates to death, came to the conclusion that democracy should be given up, that government should be confined to a self-perpetuating élite who should be stripped of all personal attachments and not permitted to have a private family life or to hold property. He came to believe that only if men had no individual interests could they govern in the general interest—if they had family interests they would practise nepotism; if they had property they would govern in the interest of their class. Many of Plato's proposals have been taken over in Great Britain by the Civil Service and the Fellows of the two old universities whose education and conduct is modelled in part upon Platonic standards and in part upon the judiciary of the Western world. However, the people of democratic countries have rejected Plato's assumption that people must be stripped of private interests before they can be permitted to govern or take part in political affairs. His view is so contrary to human nature, so contrary to the ordinary impulses of man that it has properly been judged as impractical. Democracy does not create a self-perpetuating élite; rather it affords citizens full participation in the selection of those parties and personalities who in their judgment are best fitted to administer the affairs of the nation.

But the problem which Plato posed remains. How, in the midst of a society consisting of powerful private interests, can you use these private interests for the general welfare, and not have the general welfare used to help a particular set of private interests? Let me begin by saying that I think that our greatest difficulty in this matter, in the United States, arises out of the high cost of political campaigns. I do not know how much it costs to run for office in Canada, but it is very expensive in the United States. For example, I ran for Alderman in 1939—my first experience in seeking elective office. I began with the naïve assumption that the voters of my ward would immediately recognize my distinction and without effort on my part would elect me by an overwhelming vote. I thought I was going to *stand* for office, as the British properly say, and that election would come to me without dust or sweat upon my part. It took only a day for me to discover that this was a fallacy. I thought I was well known in the country, but I discovered that I was not well known in my ward. Furthermore the fact that I was a college professor did not help me at all, even in a University ward. Quite the contrary; it was a detriment, particularly among the people who liked to go to taverns and saloons. Therefore, I began to be active and I started *walking*, not standing for office, going around shaking hands with people. I soon discovered that this was not enough, that I must speed up the tempo. So I began to *run* for office. I think that the difference in verbs is representative of the difference in tempo: the British *stand* for office, but the Americans *run* for office—and I ran very hard! I quickly discovered that the expenses of a headquarters, of telephones, of posters, of literature, of halls, and so on—all legitimate expenses—amounted to a great deal of money. Before it was over, the cost of this election—without my personal expenses—came to $10,000. Now, $5,000 was given by my friends and students but I had to give $5,000 myself. The election was supposed to be non-partisan, but I was supported by my party, the Democratic party, and I think they spent about $20,000. My opponents, I have good reason to believe, spent about $40,000. The job paid $5,000.

Once in office I was deluged with requests to contribute to church year books, to buy tickets to church socials. Representatives of churches would call and imply that it would be a very good thing if I contributed, that if I did not contribute this would be remembered. Finally, I had to have a sheet mimeographed: "Please help me to be an honest alderman." On it I explained that if I made all these contributions I would either have to go into the racket, so to speak, or get out of politics. I concluded, "I do not think you would wish to contribute to the delinquency of an alderman." As representatives of these churches would come and ask me to buy tickets, I would give them this sheet of paper and have them read it. You could see their faces fall as they read on. Fortunately, the war came and so I did not have to run for re-election in that ward.

I do not know how much it costs to be elected as United States Senator; according to a curious law in the United States candidates for the Senate can spend only $25,000. In a state which has ten and a half million people—which is the population of my state of Illinois: a little over half the population of Canada—$25,000 is not a large sum. Thus, in the populous states and in the national campaign those of us who run for office do the only thing we can do. Our friends set up separate committees which solicit and pay out the funds. We are very careful not to know how much money they raise or spend. In fact I have to sign a statement that I do not know what are the monies, and in order to sign that statement truthfully, I cannot know. Speaking not from personal knowledge, but merely from general belief, I would say that it would cost a minimum of $200,000 to stage an adequate campaign for the Senate in the State of Illinois. I would imagine that in New York State it would cost a minimum of half a million dollars. I would think that to be elected Mayor of Chicago would cost somewhere between one-half to one million dollars. In the Presidential campaign, of course, the cost runs into millions upon millions of dollars. But though these are huge sums they need not involve any illegitimate expenses whatsoever.

Ideally, the money should be raised by small contributions from large numbers of people—contributions sufficiently small so that the candidate or the party will not be deeply indebted to any one person, and so that various strata in the population are represented. Formerly the number of small contributors was relatively slight. But the picture has been changing in recent years. My party, for instance, has on occasion given a series of dinners—$100 dinners, $50 dinners, $25 dinners, $10 dinners, and, out in the small towns, $5 dinners. This is a means of making people feel they are getting something for their money and at the same time helping a good cause. The result is that parties are more democratically and universally financed than in the past. But still I think it is true that, in general, the small contributions of the many form a relatively slight fraction of the total amount of money spent. In the main, the money still comes from the big contributors. Some of them are idealists who give because they believe in the candidate's principles (although these can be troublesome upon occasion, later). Some are the "sports" who simply like to see candidates run as they like to see horses run, and are willing to take a flyer, so to speak, on some candidate (these can be very precious fellows for the candidate to have on his side, because they never make requests afterwards). But most of the so-called contributors are not contributors at all; they are investors. They invest in a party or a candidate and expect to be paid back afterwards in the form of special favours or in legislation. This, of course, puts tremendous pressure upon the parties and upon the legislators, and is one of the habits which we need to change. We need to universalize party and personal support to a much greater degree. I think, also, that radio and television should donate a much larger share of time than they have given in the past. In the last United States election the networks did give, for the first time, free time for the four debates between the candidates for President. Our radio and television people seem to overlook the fact that they are using airways which belong to the public, airways which have been given to them without charge and from which millions of dollars of profits and more millions of wealth have been accumulated. At the same time, the requirement or the unwritten rule that 15 per cent of their time should be given for public purposes is really honoured in the breach far more than in the observance. I feel that the radio and television groups should be prepared to make a much greater contribution of free time, at least to the two major parties—or to any candidate or party which polls 10 per cent of the votes.

If we are not able to base our parties more broadly, we may be driven, in the comparatively near future, to a reform which Theodore Roosevelt proposed and which has in part been adopted in Japan and Puerto Rico—financing the cost of the campaigns out of the public treasury. In Puerto Rico, in a community of two-and-a-quarter million people, the parties are given $150,000 for their campaign, and this is given to the minority parties on equal terms. Japan provides similar financing. Since, in any event, the public now pays indirectly after the election for the cost of the campaign, in the form of special privileges which are granted, I think it would be much better and cleaner if it paid directly, a limited amount, before the campaign. Then the contributions of individuals would take the form of working, and giving time rather than money.

Now let me turn to some of the problems which a legislator or an administrative official confronts after he is elected. One of them is the danger of being put under obligation to private individuals and interests. Perhaps I may be allowed another personal illustration. After I was elected in 1948, presents began to descend upon my wife and me. Almost every hour, the postman or expressman would come up several flights of stairs to our apartment bearing gifts. The most common gift would be a bottle of whisky, but on occasion there were cases of whisky, bolts of silk—no fur coats, but promises of fur coats. The most subtle gift of all was an eighteen-volume work on the art and architecture of Italy; someone had found out my weak spot and gone directly to it. The presents poured in until they filled almost a whole room. My wife and I decided that these were not gifts—that, in the main, these were sent to us to put us under an obligation and that we would probably find the donors turning up shortly as seekers after favour. So, after repacking everything, we sent them back to the donors—collect!

We thought we had solved the problem. But as soon as I got to Washington the presents began arriving all over again. I found that I was spending a good deal of my time asking myself: "Will I, should I accept this? Should I turn that down?" This was taking up a disproportionate amount of my time, and I found that I was not able to work on the problems that were much more important. I then decided to draw a line. Presents above this line I would not accept, presents below the line, if sent with reasonably honest intent, I would accept —and I fixed the limit at two dollars and a half. I have to admit that the two dollar and a half limit does excite people's laughter, as it probably does yours. In this connection I remember a collector of revenue for the Richmond district who was up before one of our Congressional committees. He said that round about the time he collects the taxes in the spring of the year, the presents would pour upon him, particularly Virginia hams. He said, "Some of these I accept and some of these I reject." A Congressman on the committee asked, "But where do you draw the line?" He replied, "I generally draw the line at 12 pounds." And everyone burst into laughter. Well, I draw the line at two dollars and a half. My friends say this suggests that I might be tempted by a present worth two dollars and 51 cents, but could resist the temptation of $2.49. I reply, you have to draw the line somewhere. Mine saves time. I merely have my secretary appraise the gifts, and it's done more or less automatically. I don't think you can corrupt a Senator for less than $2.50.

A good many public officials have accepted gifts, entertainment, and so on, until gradually they come under personal obligation to the donor. I believe it was Aristotle who said that one of the essential features of ethics is reciprocity and mutuality. Those accepting gifts feel obligated to the donor and soon he appears before them perhaps as an attorney, perhaps as a lobbyist, and it is very easy for them to pay off a private obligation at the public's expense. One of the saddest cases I know concerned the son of a friend of mine who became the Chief Attorney for the Internal Revenue Department. His salary was small, only $10,000, and he began accepting gifts and trips to Florida, trips to New York and so forth. Lo and behold, the people who were so generous to him soon began to appear in tax cases, and he began to make rulings in their favour. These dealings came out and he had to resign. He became a clerk in a grocery store, and a few years ago committed suicide. Another unhappy case involved a man who started out as U.S. Attorney in Charlotte, North Carolina. He testified later that he would drive down to the Court House in Charlotte and leave the side window of his car open. During the day anonymous people would come along and throw presents into the back of the car and in the evening he would find the car filled. In return for his fine work in Charlotte he was promoted to Assistant Attorney General in Washington, put in charge of the Criminal Division and the Tax Division, and he still followed the policy of keeping windows of his car open and accepting gifts. He is at present, I think, serving a Federal term. (It does not invalidate my point if I say frankly that the particular offence for which he was charged and served a term was one of which I think he was relatively innocent. If I had been on the jury in this particular case, I would not have voted to convict him. I think that on other charges, probably, he could have been convicted, but not on the particular one.)

A public official should beware of putting himself under obligation to any private person: he must walk alone just as a baseball umpire must walk alone. This is an especially difficult rule for an elected official, because he cannot give the impression that he is a snob or prig. He must also be man-of-the-world and, within limits, hail-fellow-well-met. How to be a part of the world and yet be independent of the world is a very difficult question to answer. The corollary is clear: a public official should live simply, very simply, unless he has ample private means of his own. And even then he should probably live simply.

We are worried in the United States, as Plato was worried long ago, over the problem of conflicts of interests. We have rigid statutes to the effect that no appointed official can hold public office and at the same time try to sell any goods to the Government. I think that, on the whole, this is a good rule. It is sometimes violated in spirit and one of the worst abuses has developed with retired defence officers of high standing. I initiated an investigation which disclosed that there were over 750 retired military officials—from the rank of army captain and above—who were on the payroll of the 100 leading defence contractors, some of them with extremely high salaries. While in many cases these men were there for technical reasons, to aid in the design and production of equipment, I am confident that in many cases they were there because it was felt that they would have a distinct influence in obtaining contracts on favourable terms. I am now engaged in a struggle to change the basis of awarding many of the contracts.

Yet Congress, in my opinion, is subject to criticism in that while we impose standards upon administrative officers, we do not impose these standards upon ourselves. There are no conflict of interest statutes so far as legislators are concerned, and I admit that it would be difficult to draw them. Nevertheless, I find myself shocked when I discover some of my colleagues who have huge amounts of money invested in particular industries not only voting for but taking an active part in the passage of legislation which deals intimately with the fortunes of that industry. I think that they should at least disqualify themselves from voting in these matters and I hope that an awakened public feeling will effect this. The problem can come up in many ways, large and small. My wife and I, for instance, do not have large resources; however, once, when the Senate was considering legislation dealing with the steel industry, the thought flitted across my mind that I owned 100 shares of U.S. Steel. This very thought served as a danger signal to me. I voted against the steel industry, in this particular case. I had never had such a reaction before because our own holdings were so slight. But we disposed of our holdings and put them into investment trusts; here the holdings are so distributed that you never know what they are, and any one act of yours would have very little effect upon them.

We have been having a good deal of discussion in the United States over the conscience and ethics of our quasi-judicial bodies—our regulatory bodies. We have great natural monopolies in the railways, the electric light companies, the gas companies. In these fields we rejected public ownership—

which I suppose Plato might have advocated—and retained private ownership but with public regulation. We went on from this to the communication industry and to aviation. Then in order to preserve competition we passed the Federal Trade Commission Act in the administration of Woodrow Wilson, and the Securities and Exchange Commission Act in the administration of Franklin D. Roosevelt. When the latter legislation was before the Banking and Currency Committee one immaculately clad Harvard man rose to say that if security dealers were required to tell the truth about the stocks and bonds which they issue, the security business would be ruined. I cannot help but think that if telling the truth would ruin the security business things must have been very bad indeed. In due course this legislation was passed and we then went on to implement the principle of the right of men to join unions and to bargain collectively with their employers in the National Labour Relations Board Act.

These quasi-judicial bodies are supposed to be independent of the President, and to represent both political parties. Nearly all start out in a spirit of reform. The sponsors of the original legislation almost never get on them, because they have usually been discredited in the process of getting the reforms (if you want to make yourself unpopular in the world, advocate something that is good for mankind!). As time wears on, the public tends to lose its interest in the reforming activity, and unfortunately those who stand out to defend the public interest may be smeared. A taste for blondes, too much drinking, unpopular political sympathies: all these things have been and are used to discredit public officials on these quasi-judicial bodies who try to defend the general interest. The conformists, on the other hand, seem to advance and prosper. In this process some officials get tired, some lose their reputation, some are seduced by the flesh-pots and resign to enter the pay of those groups which, presumably, they have been regulating. There has been a progressive degeneration of these administrative tribunals in the last fifteen years. In all honesty, I have to admit that it went on when my own party was in power, as well as during the following eight years. In the main, these quasi-judicial bodies, instead of regulating the industries they were supposed to regulate, have been controlled and regulated by them. And in addition to this, some unethical practices have developed. Individuals have formed the habit of appearing in the offices of these men and making representations they would not make in public. The cocktail party is a place where many of these conversations can occur. (This activity is not supposed to exist in the field of judiciary, but it apparently does. I was once chairman of a committee on Ethics and Government of the Senate and I invited Judge Learned Hand, probably our most distinguished judge, to testify. I said to him: "Justice Hand, I am sure that no one ever approaches you about a case which is on trial before you; no one approaches you in the Court Room." He looked at me with a pitying expression and replied: "Senator, this happens more frequently than you believe.") Members of these administrative tribunals move socially with a group of people who can either bring pressure on or make suggestions to them. I think, however, that we are moving to make it a matter of public record in the near future that any conversations which are held outside of the hearing room will be recorded completely. There is a special requirement for legislators in this connection too, because sometimes we are asked by our constituents to try and get a favourable ruling. This is improper. It is proper, of course, that a subject be given speedy consideration and fair consideration, but quite improper to ask for a decision in any one particular field.

We have, as you know, heavy income taxes and heavy corporation taxes. In practice, however, the severity of these taxes is greatly reduced by loopholes which have been found in the tax laws and in the administration of these laws. The result is that people with equal incomes will pay vastly different taxes depending upon whether or not they are in a favoured position. For example, we have a withholding tax on wages and salaries but we do not have a withholding tax on dividends and interest. The Internal Revenue Bureau reports that seven billion dollars of taxable dividends and interest are paid out and never reported; upon these, therefore, no taxes are paid. One of the tax reforms which some of us are trying to get adopted is a provision that there should be equal treatment of dividends and interest and wages and salaries and withholding tax should be applied to both. We believe that this could raise at least one billion dollars a year more in revenue.

There is another practice of evasion which is pretty close to being a racket—the liberal use of expense accounts listed in tax returns as business expense. On one occasion when I was driving in Fort Lauderdale in Florida I noticed the harbour full of private yachts, and was told that every one of these yachts was charged as a business expense—their owners invite business guests and charge their entertainment to their business firm. This is carried to ridiculous extremes and my country is rapidly becoming an expense-account civilization. In all fairness one has to add that the same thing is said to be true in Great Britain.

If we could stop these practices, I think we would raise from three to five billion dollars a year of additional revenue, and this would permit us to finance the social programme of the new administration, and also to reduce the taxes on the upper income brackets.

The basic problem in democratic civilization, as has been said, is the problem of defending the diffused general interest of people as consumers and taxpayers against the concentrated private interests of special groups. We have what is probably the most powerful industry on the Continent intent on maintaining what I think is an unjust tax favour, the gas and oil depletion allowance, which results in that industry paying only one-third the rate of taxes of other industries. The oil and gas industry is powerful, has billions of dollars of resources, and has great weapons for creating a favourable public opinion. The diffused interest of the general taxpayer, in this particular instance, is slight. An increase in gas rates does not mean many dollars to any individual family but it does mean 600 million dollars a year to the industry. When a diffused general interest comes in conflict with a concentrated private interest, the general interest tends to lose.

More than anything else the need in our democracy is for defenders of the general interest. The best defenders of general interest in the United States are the women, and the League of Women Voters is a most admirable organization. Other women's organizations are also very staunch. Some of the industrial unions—notably the United Automobile Workers—have seen this problem and have realized that to protect their people they should try to get not only higher wages but also lower prices. We need more great newspapers on this continent; I think there has been a steady decline of the press during the last seventy-five years. And above all we need political leaders who, despite all the difficulties which attend modern life, are willing to deal honestly with the issues and continue to defend the general interest by openly debating these matters before the public.

9 / Religious Ethics and Foreign Policy

JOHN C. BENNETT

There are two religious convictions which underlie all that any of us can say from faith about the ethics that should control foreign policy. The first is the affirmation that God is the Lord of the nation, of all nations. As the prophet known as the Second Isaiah said (40:17): "All the nations are as nothing before him, they are accounted by him as less than nothing and emptiness." And as Amos said much earlier (9:7): "Did I not bring up Israel from the land of Egypt, and the Philistines from Caphtor and the Syrians from Kir?" The belief that all of the nations are under the judgment and the providence and the mercy of God is central to Biblical thought. Since it is the nation that so easily becomes the ultimate object of loyalty for its citizens, this faith that God transcends the nation is always a warning against national idolatry. And it is national idolatry or the idolatry of a human group or system that is the greatest obstacle to the tolerance and humaneness which are the conditions for decent relations among the nations, conditions which have seldom seemed as remote as in this hour.

Close to this conviction about the transcendence and sovereignty of God is the teaching about the persistence of sinful pride and self-centredness on all levels of human life, not least on the level of high moral achievements and often most of all on the level of national or ideological loyalty. This is a warning against what we might call covert idolatry, not the explicit worship of the nation as God, but the assumption that God is always on our side.

As we look at the Communist nations we may well be concerned by the fact that they recognize no God above them and seem to make a god out of the Communist scheme or the Communist goal and, provisionally perhaps, out of the party or the state. But it is our temptation to assume that, because our opponents are atheists, God must be on our side and to overlook the extent to which Communism itself is a judgment upon the sins and failure of the middle-class world. The very atheism of Communism is a judgment upon the churches which for so long were unconcerned about the victims of the industrial revolution and early capitalism and which have usually been ornaments of the *status quo* no matter how unjust it has been. The temptation to turn the cold war into a holy crusade is ever with us and, in so far as we yield to it, we make impossible the tolerance and humaneness which must yet come into international relations if there is to be a future for mankind.

One of the questions which I find most troublesome is this: how can we relate the high and sensitive ethics of the Bible, the ethic of love and humility which Christians find central in the New Testament (though they do not forget that the two great commandments are quoted from the Old Testament and they do not claim that they have any monopoly on Christian love or that they exemplify it very well), to the issues of foreign policy, to all of the problems of power, of deterrence, of conflict that fill every day's newspapers?

At the heart of Christian ethics is emphasis upon dynamic love. It involves caring for all neighbours for their dignity and their welfare. It involves love for enemies and not merely love for those who love us. It involves self-spending and sacrifice without limits. It involves going to the ends of the earth to serve the neighbour there in so far as is possible. It involves forgiveness—forgiving seventy times seven. It involves a special caring for those whom the world neglects or exploits or condemns, for the lost sheep. How in God's name can we relate such an ethic as this to national policies or, in the midst of the cold war, policies which Christian citizens may find that they must support, or else recommend other policies which raise the same question in principle even though they may seem more tolerable?

My answer—admittedly not as good as I should like—is as follows: There is no Christian foreign policy, as such, but Christians under the pressure of their faith must seek policies which are most likely to promote justice and freedom and peace, that have the best chance of enabling neglected people everywhere to be raised to a new level of dignity and opportunity. At any given moment the alternatives that are available may be very few and each of them may have repellent elements.

It is always possible for the individual Christian or for Christian groups to say that the alternatives are so bad that the best that can be done is to oppose them all and choose a vocation that involves witness to the love of God by word and deed, often by suffering, which bypasses the immediate political issue. Whether or not he starts with the kind of ethical absolutism which conditions us for such a position, any Christian may find himself faced with a choice between such evil and hopeless political alternatives that he might feel compelled to choose this special vocation of non-political witness. In the situation today, however, most of us have to stay conscientiously with one of the available political alternatives. Even a nuclear pacifist in Canada or the United States has to have in mind a second-best policy for the government because the United States government—and I speak only of that—cannot be expected to choose the way of unilateral nuclear disarmament which is what nuclear pacifism implies. It would be psychologically and politically impossible for the government to choose a policy which would leave the Communist world with a monopoly of the most decisive form of power. Indeed, I do not think that we ought to permit a monopoly of nuclear power in the Communist world even if it proved to be psychologically and politically possible to do so. The need of power is a given element of which ethics must take account.

Ethics and National Interest

I am never satisfied by the way in which anyone deals with this subject. And I have never been able to arrive at an adequate formulation myself. But here I shall make an attempt. Our thought should move between two poles, one of which is that government is a trustee for the national interest. Those who lead the nation can stretch the conception of the national interest so that what is done in the name of national interest can also be supported out of a genuine concern for the welfare of other nations. The interest of a nation has value in itself as long as it is not made supreme; it has to do with the well being of as many million neighbours as there are and the nation as such has its own distinctive contribution to make to humanity. The other pole is the recognition that no citizen, whether he be Christian or Jew or a man of conscience who adheres to no traditional religion, should make national interest ultimate for himself or for his actions and decisions as a citizen.

It is difficult to do justice to both of these poles. There are some considerations which may be helpful in many circumstances, however. The first is, as George Kennan and Hans

Morgenthau have pointed out, that a prudent concern for the national interest often has great moral value as a limiting concept. A nation that crusades for moral ideas that are not consistent with its long-term interest is likely to throw its weight about far too much, to act as though it knew what was good for every other nation. At this moment of world history, restraint in the use of power is often highly moral even when it is only the restraint of prudence. Morgenthau describes the extreme belief that "What is good for the crusading country is by definition good for all mankind, and if the rest of mankind refuses to accept such claims to universal recognition, it must be converted with fire and sword."[1] A nation that is controlled by ideology may never limit its goals. A nation guided by a prudent sense of national interest may at least be willing to accept limits. Do not we all hope that the time may come when we can be sure that the Russians will be so involved in their own affairs that they will be less motivated by the ideological impulse to remake the world?

A second consideration is that the real solidarity of mankind means that we can often act for the sake of mutual interests. The United States can quite sincerely aid India for the sake of the people of India and at the same time for the sake of a common human concern to enable India to find a way forward that is favourable to peace and spiritual freedom in the whole world. Often this emphasis upon mutual interest is better than the emphasis upon sheer generosity, for the latter may beget cynicism and resentment. There are times for heedless generosity despite the behaviour of nations—as for example the efforts of many nations to meet the needs of the people of Chile after a most destructive earthquake. If a nation is to act in terms of what I have called mutual interests based upon the solidarity of mankind, however, the sights of the people have to be lifted. If the nation as a whole is to be guided by

[1] Hans Morgenthau, *In Defense of National Interest* (New York: Alfred Knopf and Co., 1951), p. 37.

a broad rather than a narrow view of national interest, there must be many people whose concern and imagination transcend all thought of national interest in their identification with the other nations who may be affected by what is done.

A third consideration is that it is in the best interests of a nation for its people to be able to live with their consciences. This leads us away from the usual conceptions of national interest altogether, for it involves matters of faithfulness to commitments to other nations or commitments to the U.N. It is also a factor when we contrast the wealth of the United States and Canada with the poverty of half of the world. Something like this is suggested by George Kennan when he says: "We should conduct ourselves at all times in such a way as to satisfy our own ideas of morality. But let us do this as a matter of obligation to ourselves, and not as a matter of obligation to others."[2] It seems to me, however, that our obligation to others must surely be a part of any morality which creates an obligation to ourselves. Nevertheless it is interesting to see one of the leading proponents of the emphasis on national interest here pointing beyond national interest.

I come back now to the implications of my second pole: the fact that the citizen should not make national interest ultimate for himself. The relations between people transcend the relations between governments. The citizen may also be a churchman, a scientist, an artist, or a friend with ties in other countries. A nation or government should want to encourage these ties, should seek to strengthen the non-political relationships between people across national boundaries. Both churches and synagogues, as part of their essential nature, participate in these non-political relationships. Much may be done by the citizens of one country for the citizens in another country which has nothing to do with national interest. In

[2]George Kennan, *Realities of American Foreign Policy* (Princeton: Princeton University Press, 1957), p. 47.

meeting major national problems, intergovernmental activity is often necessary because of the vast scale of the problems. Yet, this should not make any less important the more personal and more flexible things that can be done across national boundaries by voluntary groups. One of the great human losses, whenever totalitarian governments are in control of a nation, is that all of these personal and voluntary relationships are suspected of having a political purpose and are restricted or entirely forbidden.

The Responsibility of Wealth

The second issue is the responsibility of the rich nations of the West to the nations which are economically poor and technically underdeveloped. That word, "underdeveloped," is a poor word and it is permissible to use it at all only if we add an adverb. I have already referred to this issue in discussing national interest because there is a point here where national interest coincides with a religious and moral imperative. But there should be something else. Karl Barth, in a passage in which he describes the marks of what he calls "cohumanity," mentions mutual help as one, and says that another is that what we do for one another we do "gladly." Surely this is relevant to our discussion here. It is not enough to say: our freedom depends upon the capacity of countries in Asia and Africa and Latin America to find the way to freedom. That needs to be said when we are asking Congress to make appropriations and it is not said to deceive Congress; it is said because it is true. Nor is it enough to say: we must live with our consciences and we are grimly determined to help other nations because we hate to look at their poverty, which pains us when we see it as tourists, or in our illustrated journals, or on our television screens. There is another dimension that is natural to our humanity, especially if we are made sensitive by our response to the love of God who loves all men. Should we not gladly share our abundance? Should we not gladly participate in the struggles of other nations to find their way to economic plenty and justice and political freedom?

Two considerations, both of which have political implications, should be emphasized. The first is that we must be open-minded about the economic and social experiments of those nations trying to do in a few years or decades what we have done on this continent over a period of several generations. Some conservatives in the United States assume that when any nation adopts any new programme that is in some degree socialistic or belongs to the pattern of the welfare state, it is therefore a stepping-stone to Communism. What they do not know is that these measures are necessary antidotes to Communism. A dogmatic individualism colours in varying degrees the minds of many people on this continent, not least the minds of Protestants, and incapacitates them for understanding the problems of these other countries. When this dogmatic individualism is combined with the influence of powerful business interests on government, the difficulty is compounded.

The second consideration is that we should not seek to make satellites of any of these nations. One very great gain in American foreign policy in recent years—and events in Cuba should not be allowed to obscure it—is that at last we have come to respect the role of neutral nations. We now seem to realize that the ideal is not two solid blocs of nations but many nations that are resolved to be free, many of them free from dependence upon either side in the cold war. We may believe that to some extent this freedom of the neutrals is made possible because the Communist world does not have a monopoly of military power. But it still remains true that it should be our concern to help nations find their own way to freedom, to be glad when they do this even if they are not allied diplomatically and militarily with us. To have many independent centres of national vitality and of moral and social and political health is much to be desired, and should be borne in mind when we say "no strings attached" to programmes of foreign aid. "No strings attached" does not mean that we are not greatly concerned that, whatever aid is provided, it reach the people within the country who need it most and not merely make the rich richer. In detail, it may be difficult to make the distinction between "strings" and conditions of the kind that have to do with greater social justice within a country. But we must try to do it.

The Problem of Co-existence

The final issue, of course, is the problem of co-existence between the Communist world and our own. In my opinion, the very fact that the world is not completely bi-polar may help to make co-existence possible. There are those who say that we should not co-exist, presumably meaning that we should subordinate the concern to prevent nuclear war to the task of resisting Communism, and that it is not enough to contain Communism but we must seek a complete victory in the cold war. Any other purpose or policy seems to them to be a case of "making peace with oppression" and is a betrayal of morality.

To all such people I say that one element in the moral life is the kind of prudence that seeks to prevent the greater evil and that their view of the cold war will almost certainly lead to hot war and to the nuclear catastrophe which will add to the victims of tyranny scores and perhaps hundreds of millions of new victims of war. Also, I say to them that the institutions of freedom in which they claim to believe so fervently are not likely to survive such a war. The survivors will be too much concerned about mere existence to give much thought to freedom. At least, so it may be. Whenever people say to me: "give me liberty or give me death" and from these noble words deduce a cold war policy that is likely to lead to a nuclear catastrophe, I say: If such a war should come, liberty will probably not survive and as for death, it is not only your death that is involved but the death of countless people who never made this choice.

I would make three suggestions about this deep and dangerous conflict in the world. First, I suggest that we try to distinguish in our minds and even in our hearts between our opposition to Communism as a faith and an ideology and a political system on the one hand, and our attitude towards those nations in which Communism is well established, on the other. Here I refer primarily to the Soviet Union. I also refer to China, but I have much less confidence in what we should do about it, except that to refuse to recognize it is the worst possible policy. In the Soviet Union at least, we are dealing with a society that has moved beyond the worst elements of the revolution and of the Stalinist terror, with people who have remarkable achievements to their credit, with a generation that is more interested in building the new society in Russia than in world revolution, even though there is still a troublesome and highly effective foreign policy designed to promote the ends of international Communism, with Communist leaders who have learned at least one thing of vast importance for us, that nuclear war would be a catastrophe for their country as well as for the capitalistic countries to which they are opposed. We should also realize that one element in Russian feeling about us is the fear that the United States may at some point in the future attack the Soviet Union. One of the results of our violent hostility to Communism is that it would be difficult for people in Russia not to think that, if we ever had a chance, we would destroy Communism in Russia. I know that no responsible person in North America today has any such intention but it would not be strange if the Russians still had this fear. We are opposed to Communism as a faith and as an ideology and as a political system, and we will do what we can to keep any Communist nation from imposing Communism upon any other nation but we can still distinguish between Communism, as such, and the Soviet Union as a nation, or China as a nation. What hope we have for the people in the Soviet Union or in China must be hope for developments within their societies, not hope that we may be able to displace Communism in either country by an external attack or by encouraging counter-revolution. We should not be engaged in the Chinese Civil War.

Secondly, I believe that we should accept with full seriousness the fact that Communist power is not primarily military power, that the cold war is not primarily a military conflict. It is true that military power has been used to extend Communism, that Communism in eastern Europe is chiefly the result of external pressure with the Red Army a continuing factor. But the areas where Communism is today the greatest threat are areas where economic and social problems cry for quick solutions and where governments are weak and unstable. Communism is one way of bringing about needed changes—a costly way which we would avoid. The attraction of Communist society in Russia may well be far more important than the persuasiveness of ideology. The power of Communism to win devoted followers who help prepare their countries for revolution is the power of an idea and of a promise and not the might of Soviet rockets. Some nations will be saved from Communism only if they see and develop alternatives to it. How often must it be said that the failure of the comfortable nations to realize the depth of the neglected social problems of half the world is the chief ally of Communism in the cold war? Unless we do realize this very soon our military power and our alliances will be of little avail. I believe that this is understood by President Kennedy and many of his associates but there are departments of our government in which it is still assumed that the conflict is primarily military and many powerful forces on this continent do not know that social revolution is a moral necessity, that it is neither right nor possible to prop up the old order. One of the most appalling aspects of the abortive attempt to stimulate a revolt in Cuba against Castro was the belief that the Cubans would rally to a standard set up by conservative exiles.

My third suggestion is that we should take a more balanced view of the risks involved in the nuclear arms race than has generally been characteristic of western governments and of public opinion—though here, as in many other matters, there are differences of emphasis in Canada and the United States. It is not sufficient to stress the risk that the Soviet Union may gain some advantage in the arms race; it is just as important to stress the risk of the arms race itself to all humanity. For a time the balance of terror, the process of mutual deterrence, has been effective in preventing war but it is false to be led from this fact to the expectation that if we are sufficiently vigilant in keeping up the deterrent power on our side, we will continue to preserve the peace for another decade.

At the moment it seems that Russian intransigence may prevent progress even in the one matter of nuclear tests. But it is necessary to remember that only a short time ago the United States government was divided within itself on the desirability of ending nuclear tests. Now we must be sure that on our side governments and negotiators are sincere and are resolved to do everything in their power to secure agreements on which arms control as a stage in disarmament can be based. If we do not admit at the start that, necessary as it is to have inspection and policing of agreements, there is no absolute security to be gained from any such process, in the effort to secure absolute security in methods of control we are likely to drift into the insecurity of the unlimited arms race. In this situation it seems futile to engage in religious or ethical exhortations which will be heard by only one side. Yet we must continue to say to all who will listen that the control of the arms race is essential not only to the physical survival of most of humanity but also to the survival of the best things which our very armaments are intended to defend. We must pray that the stalemate may be broken and that a fresh start may soon become possible.

Finally, the relation of religion to this conflict between the Communist and non-Communist worlds should be considered. The more that the religious conflict can be distinguished from the international conflict, the better. The international conflict results in separation of peoples and in hostility. The conflict between Communism on the one hand, and Christianity and Judaism on the other, is compatible with relationships between peoples and with works of love. If there can develop a structure of co-existence between the nations on both sides of the conflict, then there will remain a struggle for the minds and souls of people, and our chief weapon in this struggle will be witness in word and in life to the truth that we have seen. Meanwhile, we in the churches and synagogues of North America can prepare ourselves for this witness by overcoming in ourselves and in our institutions the deep bias that we find there in favour of the *status quo*. When we make clear to ourselves that our own tradition should ally us with the forces of social revolution, we will be in a better position to help those who have been the victims of the dominance of the western, white, middle-class world to find channels for this revolution favourable to the freedom of mind and spirit.

10 / The Ethical Necessity of Defending Democracy

PAUL H. DOUGLAS

The desire to preserve freedom and to extend it, and our common heritage from English culture, is the great contribution of the West to civilization. But it is well to remember a remark of George Washington's at Valley Forge: "Men will hold this freedom lightly when they no longer have to die to preserve it." In the years since the conclusion of World War II, we have found this very true. Our belief in freedom helped us through one period of testing, when it seemed as if that freedom might vanish from the earth. We were successful in defending it and fortunately with not many untoward results inside our own countries. Regrettably, we have settled back again to accept and to take for granted the precious things which we have saved. To my mind, however, the preservation and extension of freedom is the supreme ethical duty for the people of the world and in particular the people of the Western world. This freedom has largely, although not wholly, descended from the British people—coming down through the struggle under Charles I in the Commonwealth for the liberties of men, the glorious revolution of 1688, which put the liberal tradition uppermost in England, the Era of Toleration of the seventeenth and eighteenth centuries culminating in the period of science and the period of enlightenment in which the American Revolution occurred. I would even include in this tradition the French Revolution itself. Finally came the struggles in the nineteenth century to establish greater political and industrial freedom.

Twenty-odd years ago this freedom was threatened by the Nazis and was nearly destroyed. We now take our victory for granted but at one time, in the early summer of 1942, the issue was very much in the balance. Had it not been for the victory of Montgomery at El Alamein, the heroic stand of the Russians at Stalingrad, and, in a very minor fashion, the American victory at Guadalcanal, the tide might well have swept over us. We are now threatened with an equal danger in the totalitarian forces of Communism. By this, I do not mean the ideology of Communism, but the system of Communism as a power which crushes out all opposition within a country and seeks by subversion and conquest to draw successive nations under its control, with its ultimate aim control over the world itself, and its chief enemy the United States of America and the free peoples of the Western world. One of the great decisions which we must make today is whether freedom is still worth defending and, if so, how should it be defended?

We need to emphasize what some of the elements of this freedom are: the freedom to worship in the church of one's choice, or, if one so desires, not to worship; the freedom to speak one's mind as long as there is no direct incitement to violence; the freedom, as an adult, to read what one desires, to go to the plays one prefers, to listen to whatever radio or television programme is available; the freedom of association with others, in fraternal groups, in unions, as long as these groups do not plan the violent overthrow of the government; freedom to discuss, to try to discover the truth, and through the freedom of the press and of association to try to propagate the truth as one sees it; freedom from arbitrary arrest; the right to reasonable bail; the right of access to one's friends and relatives; the right to a public trial; the right to be represented by a lawyer; the right to be tried by a jury; the right of appeal; the right not to be punished for the sins of one's parents or the associations of one's friends; the right to vote; the right to vote by secret ballot; the right to cast one's vote for the candidates and parties of one's choice; and from this, the right of the majority to govern, but also the reciprocal right of the minority to be free to argue, to oppose the government, and to seek to become the majority by persuasion. Inherent in this is the assumption implicit in the political process that the minority gives up the right to revolution and agrees to accept the mandate of the majority. The majority, in return, tolerates the minority, permits it to function, and is willing to cede power if it is outvoted. Under this system, decisions are made basically by the people according to the information which they have and in accordance with their spiritual, moral, and economic standards. These rights and duties provide for the most peaceful form of transfer of power that we know and although the system is not, of course, perfect, it has worked better than any other.

Why are these freedoms precious? Why are they constructive? Why are they—to my mind—the best set of political principles which mankind has yet created? In the first place, the act of choice improves the character of men and women. It does so because the moral life is developed by human choice between alternatives, which in turn depends on the exercise of intelligence, of moral precision, and on the very necessity of decision. Hence, men and women who have the power of choice, and who exercise that choice, are the most interesting, the most fully developed people. Indeed I have heard theologians argue that the grant of free will to mankind by God is designed to permit men fully to develop themselves. This, I think, is perhaps the greatest advantage that democracy has. By its very process it improves the character of men and women in a way in which no dictatorship and no monolithic state can do.

The second great advantage, of course, is that the very process of discussion tends to sift truth from error. In his "Essay on Liberty," John Stuart Mill points out that if a new idea or an old idea were true, discussion and examination would cause it to be more firmly held, would entrench it more deeply, and would enable it to withstand the corrosive effects of criticism more effectively than if discussion were suppressed. If the old idea were false, its falsity could be exposed. But if, as is generally true, an old theory were partially true and partially false, and the new theory partially false and partially true, then by the process of discussion, and out of the conflict of ideas, the true features of both alternatives could be combined, or, as happens sometimes, an idea could be developed which would be not merely a synthesis of the two, but, in a sense, a completely new theory transcending the two.

In other words, democracy and freedom create what Hegel would call a dialectic of peaceful change which permits us to adapt to science, to movements of population, to new ethical concepts, without revolution. This dialectic rests on some fundamental assumptions, one of which is that people, on the whole, will be adequately informed. What a responsibility this places upon education, upon the press, upon radio, upon television, upon public communication of all kinds, for the information must not only be accurate but comprehensive. But an even more fundamental assumption is that men will ultimately make correct choices or those choices which are most nearly correct; the basic desire of the human heart is taken to be for a life of virtue. The dialectic rests, therefore, in the end upon faith and the correctness of the assumptions of the Judeo-Christian tradition.

This theory of nineteenth-century liberalism and freedom, partially developed by Milton and by Locke and more fully expounded by John Stuart Mill and by Abraham Lincoln, may seem to picture the world as it ought to be rather than as it sometimes is. It is perfectly clear that the exponents of democracy have underestimated the difficulty of modern people in knowing the truth. They have tended to disregard the frustrations in men and women which could lead them to make wicked choices, and to neglect the demonic power of evil within man which, at times, takes possession of him, evidently and completely. To read the documents concerning the Nazi concentration camps, Dachau, Auschwitz, and the others, or the story of the gassing of six million Jews or the documents concerning the exiling of hundreds of thousands of Russian peasants, who, in the middle of the winter were crowded into box-cars—men, women, and children—deprived of food and heat, and shipped thousands of miles to Siberia, many freezing to death on the way, is to be convinced of the dark powers of evil which lurk within the human breast. These atrocities were perpetrated by men who had absolute power, who had, by the power of dictatorship, shielded themselves from public knowledge of what they were doing. They thus rendered the ethical opinions of mankind relatively helpless, and were able to exercise the absolute power in their hands for evil. Yet, paradoxically enough, from this there can develop a greater belief in the values of freedom and also a greater belief in the need of decentralization so that no one person or group can have absolute power; for mankind, at present, is not capable of exercising absolute power with any degree of mercy or charity.

In my opinion, I want to repeat, we have an ethical duty to defend the system of free democracy and, if possible, to extend it. That is the basic challenge which underlies all superficial issues at the present time. How can we purify our system of democracy, remove its internal weaknesses, win the allegiance of more people to it, and protect ourselves against those who would destroy it from without? We know that there are internal weaknesses of democracy, but a democratic country is inherently self-critical and it is very fortunate that this is so. The presence of opposing political parties, the existence of a free church, of a relatively free press, all mean that internal weaknesses which develop are to some degree exposed. In a dictatorship, of course, knowledge and criticism can be suppressed and weaknesses hidden whereas the weaknesses of democracy are blazoned to the world. Unfortunately the very existence of these internal weaknesses causes people in the democratic countries to lose confidence and faith in their system, and disillusions neutrals and doubters elsewhere. There have been many reasons advanced as to why Rome fell. I think that one reason is that the Romans became tired, lost faith in their system (which did have its brutalities), lost faith in their religion, and decided that it was not worth while to defend Roman civilization against the Gothic movement from the north.

In the United States we are not as self-satisfied as we are often pictured. We are well aware, many of us, of the grave economic and moral weaknesses of our society. The worst of these is, of course, our treatment of the Negroes, who form roughly a tenth of our population, and who certainly are not treated as men and women with the inspiration of God in their hearts and as having a right to develop with social freedom. This weakness is hurting us not only inside America, but around the world as well. To go further, we have some of the most appalling slums in the world in our cities and we have badly decayed areas in the country. We have some corruption in our politics, although not as much as is commonly imagined. These are weaknesses which we must remove, in order to increase the national prestige, of course, but primarily to give people a greater incentive to defend the democratic system which, with all its faults deserves to last and spread.

It is necessary to win to the support of freedom the present neutral nations of the world. Like ancient Gaul, the world, at present, is divided into three parts—the world of Communist dictatorship, the world of democratic freedom, and the world of the neutrals. This neutral world is, in the main, composed of coloured people—black, brown, and yellow. More recently, it includes the people of Latin America. All these people are poor, living on an average income of somewhat less than $200 a year. It is difficult to maintain democracy on less than $200 a year, even to attain democracy. These people need help and one of the big tasks of the democratic nations of the West is to prove that we are really concerned with their fate.

In the sixteen years since the conclusion of World War II the United States has expended 70 billion dollars in aid to foreign nations. Never in the history of the world has any nation made such contributions to help other countries. We do not intend to reduce our effort. We are going to carry this burden—and it is going to be a burden—for many years to come, because both of the great political parties, with some exceptions, basically believe we are called upon to do so. But I submit that we cannot be expected to bear this burden alone. The needs of the world are too great for any one nation, however prosperous, however well-intended, to shoulder it exclusively. We ask for help from the other countries and the peoples of the Western world not to lessen our burden, but to demonstrate that they, too, are anxious to convince the neutral people of the world that we are their friends and that it would be far better for them and for the world itself if they ranged themselves on the side of democracy rather than Communism.

Nearly everyone will agree that we should try to defend democracy by removing its internal defects and by proving our friendship with the other peoples of the world. Now we come to a point upon which many people disagree. There can be no doubt that political Communism intends to conquer the world and to use force to do so, if necessary. This is implicit in all the teachings of the Communist leaders, from Marx to Engels to Lenin and Stalin to Khrushchev. It is also clearly indicated by the day-to-day politics and procedures of the Soviet Union and Communist China. But there are many high-minded people of character who do not believe in resisting this aggression of Communism by physical force. We should not dismiss these people as pacifists, nor hold them in contempt. The honest ones among them are deeply sincere, and they raise a profound moral issue which we need carefully to consider. They argue that physical resistance simply increases hatred, and hence even though the side you favour wins a war, the bitterness and hatred remains and bursts out in further and greater wars. They have faith that one's opponents can be won over by deeds of lovingkindness and that one should develop the spiritual force with which to conquer hostility and brutality. They also use the practical argument that passive resistance is more successful than violent resistance, and they point to the success of Gandhi and the attainment of Indian independence.

Let me deal with this question of Gandhiism first. Had the Indians carried out armed revolt against British power in India they would have been shot down and obliterated. They did not have arms, nor were they trained in using them; they were therefore in no position to revolt. They took their only weapon, passive resistance, refusing to work, refusing to eat, refusing to pay taxes. It proved to be a mighty weapon because their campaign was being carried out against a comparatively liberal modern state. It is true that the British threw Gandhi, Nehru, and thousands of others into jail; it is true that they suppressed some of the newspapers. In the main, however, Gandhi and Nehru were allowed to write and to publish, their followers were allowed to talk, they were allowed to appeal to the conscience of Great Britain and they had friends who carried their message around the world. Finally, the British conscience could not accept keeping a great people in subjection any longer, and the Labour Government, with the aid of Lord Mountbatten, freed India. In my opinion, to make use of Shakespeare's phrase for the death of the Thane of Cawdor, "Nothing in his life became him like the leaving it," nothing in the history of Great Britain so became her as the manner in which she gave up her control over India.

The United States have not done too badly either in abandoning imperialist activities. The first money I ever earned as a boy of 8 was picking blueberries and raspberries. I picked a hundred quarts, got a cent apiece, and gave 50 cents to the American Anti-Imperialist League which was then agitating for the withdrawal of American troops and the granting of independence to the Philippines and to Cuba. We have now no colonial possessions anywhere. The Platt Amendment, which gave us the right to intervene in Cuba, has been repealed. The Philippines have been granted full independence. Puerto Rico is a commonwealth and can leave at any time. Marines used to go into Haiti and Nicaragua and Santa Domingo—they will not go back. Britain and to a large degree, France are ceasing to be imperialistic powers, largely because the ethics of modern life forbid it.

But suppose a dictatorial state had controlled India? Gandhi would not only have been locked up, he would have been shot and his followers would have been killed as well. Perhaps even more important, they would not have been permitted to state their case, or to be heard, and knowledge of them would have been suppressed, as the Communists obliterated the memory of the Social revolutionaries, who were their initial partners in the government of Russia. Children might be taken away from their families, kept entirely in schools, and taught to revile their parents. Long ago I came to the conclusion that if dictatorial evil which reaches out for conquest is not actively resisted by the weapons of the flesh, mankind will be destroyed. To be reassured, we have only to ask ourselves this question: Was resistance to the Nazis justified or was it not? I think we must say that it was, for, terrible as the war was, the conquest of the free world, the universal establishment of concentration camps, and the denial of human liberties to everyone—these would have been far worse.

If resistance to Nazism was justified is not resistance to Communism? Logically, one would agree, but a new factor must be considered. World War II was, after all, conducted in a relatively primitive fashion for it was conducted in a prenuclear age. We now have the capacity, through the atomic and more particularly the hydrogen bombs, through the death ray, and through bacteriological warfare, to destroy an entire people and an entire civilization. A direct conflict between the democracies and the Communists, one argument runs, would mean universal destruction, universal contamination. Mr. Bertrand Russell has said that he would rather live under Communism than experience a nuclear war and his views are strongly supported in Great Britain, though not as strongly in the United States. If everyone comes to the same conclusion as Mr. Russell, we will, almost certainly, live under Communism. The Russians will create situation after situation, and threaten to launch a nuclear missile attack if we do not give in. If we back down each time under their threat, little by little, Russia will take over. Southeast Asia will go, then India, then the Near East. Japan will ally itself with Red China and move out of the Western alliance. Latin America will go; Berlin will be taken. There will be a general break-up of the free world, and the ultimate conquest of Great Britain, the United States, and Canada.

We must ask ourselves: do we want this to happen? Would it not be the most abhorrent development we could imagine? A life of peace and harmony and goodwill is, we know, best for the world. Many people believe it can be obtained and certainly we should try to obtain it. But we should also ask ourselves what is the worst thing that can happen to us— Would it be physical death or loss of freedom and all that this means? If we say that physical death is not the worst thing but that loss of freedom is, then there follow certain inevitable conclusions. The first is that we should not back down when we are exposed to threats, but should stand our ground. Such a resolution will be badly needed in the months and years which lie ahead when we are going to have our nerves tested as they have never been tested before. A corollary is that if we do not intend to back down, we should have a force adequate to deter others from attacking, a force giving us an ability to retaliate with nuclear weapons and to withstand peripheral probing attacks, and to put out brush-fire wars.

To do this the co-operation of all nations is needed. The world cannot depend on one or two powerful countries alone. Think back to the lessons of the 1930's. The Scandinavian countries did not arm because they thought they would be protected by the British Navy. The result was that the Nazis took Denmark in a few hours, and Norway in a few days. The Low Countries did not arm because they expected to be saved by France and England. They were overrun in a few days. France itself trusted to a purely defensive war and the incomplete Maginot Line. It was overrun in a few weeks. The rest of the world largely sat by, my own country included. For a time Britain and the dominions held alone. For her effort in that terrible year from June 1940 to December 1941, we all owe her a tremendous debt.

But in the future can most of the nations sit out and expect someone else to save their liberties for them? In my opinion, there is a tremendous necessity for pooled effort on the part of the nations which believe in freedom. Britain, the United States, Canada, Australia, New Zealand, France, the Low Countries, the Scandinavian countries, Italy, and West Germany have the major portion of the economic strength of the world. In all, they comprise close to half a billion people. If they are willing to subordinate disputes among themselves, to stand firm, to provide adequate defences and make clear that they intend to use them, then there is at least a possibility —the best one that I know of—that the Communists may not attack. We may therefore have peace for a considerable period of time, during which new forces may develop inside the captive countries, possibly inside the dictatorships themselves, which may remove a large portion of the danger.

We are told that one should never pay off a blackmailer, that one should rather resist and make it clear that one is ready for them to do their worst. When this is done, in the majority of cases, the threat is not carried through. I think this is true also in the dealings of nations. None the less, though we may be strong and ready to use our strength, let us seek peace at the same time. Let us not become a militarized people with only brutal standards, but let us value love and goodwill and let us try to practise it among ourselves and towards other people, and hope that our example may spread. This is the tremendous duty we have.

I have been reading recently Thucydides' chronicles of the Persian War. The decisions which we have to make now are no graver for us than those the little city-states had to make at the time of the Persian War. When Athens decided to resist Persia it faced the strong possibility of complete extinction at the hands of the enemy. Yet, knowing this, the Athenians chose to resist and resisting they conquered and stood. In succeeding centuries they gave to the human race beauty, philosophy, drama, art, and architecture—the most enduring and valuable heritage we have. I suggest that we should be of good courage. We should not be frightened by the danger that is now upon us—and it is very much upon us. We should appreciate the great traditions which have been created for us and under which we live and should be resolute to defend those traditions, anxious to remove our weaknesses, and to be kind and loving to others. If we do these things, the chances are in favour of our survival; if we do not do them, the whole tradition of Western freedom will be but a passing phase in the long history of mankind.

Part Four: The Jewish Contribution

BERNARD MANDELBAUM

SIMON GREENBERG

11 / Jews and the Nations of the World

BERNARD MANDELBAUM

All at once, a mournful silence enveloped the victorious army of farmers and refugees. The time: dusk. The date: the third day of the week, the twenty-fifth of Kislev, 168 B.C.E. The place: the steps of the Temple in Jerusalem. Judah Macabee and the Israelites, exultant from their conquest of the Syrian invader, were shattered by the sight of the profanation of their sanctuary. Idols and pagan symbols occupied the altar and Holy of Holies where Jews worshipped the One, Invisible God. Immediately the people set themselves to cleansing the Temple and rededicating it to God. This historic event is commemorated in the Festival of Hanukkah. However, the re-establishment of the place of worship was part of the larger task of reconstructing the Jewish state which had been under Syrian rule for three years.

The Jews, now in power and full control of the land, were faced with this major problem: What was to be the status of the Gentiles living in Judea? It was at that time that the Jewish Council formulated the "Seven Commandments of Noah" as the law of the land. Thus the prohibitions against murder, theft, cruelty to animals, sexual licence, blasphemy, worship of idols, and violation of civil justice became universal—for Gentile and Jew alike. Beyond these rules, Gentiles were free to follow their own religious or irreligious inclinations, whereas the ceremonial laws of Judaism were obligatory only on members of the Jewish faith. The Noachide Laws are thus a core of ethical principles which are binding on all the descendants of Noah, i.e., on all mankind. Christians, Moslems, Buddhists, Jews, secularists: all must accept this basic moral code. Beyond it, however, each religious group is expected to worship the Almighty in accordance with its historic traditions.

The circumstances of history under which the commandments of Noah were specifically formulated are of great significance for understanding the attitude of Judaism towards other religious groups. One might think that Jews, in later times and other places a minority group, formulated their belief in religious diversity as a result of the exigencies of their own difficulties, as a kind of "insurance policy." However, the fact that this principle, implied in the opening chapters of Genesis, was most clearly formulated when Jews were the majority and in power in Judea, underscores this truth: *Judaism views religious diversity as a principle of Creation.* Religious diversity, in its view, is a theological truth and not a sociological conclusion.

Diversity within an over-all unity characterizes all aspects of Creation—in nature and in the life of man. Consider how one star is like another, and a blade of grass seems just like another, and a snowflake seems identical with the one next to it. Indeed, the individual units in these categories of creation have a great deal in common. Yet study them, and each of the millions of stars, blades of grass, or flakes of snow is unique. Among men, as in nature, there is diversity within unity.

In the second century, the Rabbis expressed this view as follows in the Talmud: "A single man was created in the world . . . to proclaim the greatness of the Holy One, blessed is He; for man stamps many coins with the one seal and they are like one another; but the King of Kings, the Holy One, blessed is He, has stamped every man with the seal of the first man [i.e., we have a great deal in common, unity], yet no one of them is like his fellow [diversity]." (*Sanhedrin.*) In our day, Martin Buber has given voice to the same truth: "Every person born into this world represents something new, something that never existed before, something original and unique. Every single man is a new thing in the world and is called upon to fulfill his particularity in this world."

What is true of nature, of individual man, applies to groups —to religious groups, as well as cultural and national groupings. Diversity within unity is God's pattern. The brotherhood of man and its concomitant fellowship of religious groups and nations—equal but different—are not pious platitudes for twentieth-century goodwill programmes. They reflect the Jewish view of the universe from the days of the Bible to our own time.

Even a cursory review of the literature reveals the consistency of this attitude in the history of Jewish thought. In the Pentateuch, the diversity of nations is presented as part of God's plan of creation (Deut. 32:8): "When the Most High gave to the nations their inheritance, when He separated the children of men. . . ."

Throughout the prophetic period, the brotherhood of man is affirmed in the teachings of the major and minor prophets. In the third division of the Bible, the Writings, God's concern for the nations of the world is a fundamental teaching, summarized most vividly by the following passage from the book of Jonah:

Thou hast had pity on the gourd [says God to Jonah] for which thou hast not labored, neither made it grow, which came up in a night and perished in a night, and should not I have pity on

Nineveh [in Babylonia, a long-standing enemy of Judea], that great city wherein are more than six score thousand persons that cannot discern between their right hand and their left hand....

The theme of unity and diversity is expounded in many passages of Rabbinic literature as reflected in the following two illustrations:

You shall therefore keep thy statutes and thine ordinances, which if a man do he shall live by them [Lev. 18:5]. Whence is it deduced that even a Gentile who studies the Law is the equal of a High Priest? From the words "which if a *man* do he shall live by them" [Leviticus Rabbah: 49:2].

On the eighth day of the Feast of Tabernacles, seventy bullocks were offered in sacrifice on behalf of the seventy nations of the world [*Sukkah* 55B].

One of the most direct expositions of the acceptance of religious diversity is found in the writings of an outstanding German Rabbi of the eighteenth century, Jacob Emden.

It is, therefore, a customary observation with me that the man of Nazareth wrought a double kindness to the world. On the one hand he fully supported the Torah of Moses, as already shown, for not one of our sages spoke more fervently about the eternal duty to fulfill the Law. On the other hand, he brought much good to the Gentiles (if only they do not overturn his noble intention for them, as certain stupid people, who did not grasp the ultimate purpose of the New Testament have done); in fact, just recently I saw a book from the press whose author did not know himself what he had written; because, had he known what he had written, then his silence would have been more becoming than his speaking, and he would have not wasted his money nor spoiled the paper and the ink uselessly: just as among us are to be found stupid scholars who have written, not between their right hand and their left in the written, nor in the oral law, but deceive the world with a tongue that speaks arrogantly; but there are highly educated men of intelligence among the Christians, even as there are among the students of our Torah a few outstanding individuals, men of lofty erudition. For he (the man of Nazareth) forbade idol-worship and removed the image-deities, and he held the people responsible for the seven commandments, lest they be like the animals of the field; he sought to perfect them with ethical qualities that are much harder even than those of the Law of Moses (as is well known), a policy that was surely just for its own sake, since that is the straightest way to acquire good traits. . . .

These are but samplings of characteristic attitudes which found expression in Jewish literature at different periods and in various parts of the world. It is important to note that the attitude reflected in the sources quoted above represents the overwhelming trend of opinion in Jewish tradition. From time to time, however, one does find statements in Jewish literature which reflect distrust, intolerance, even hatred of other religious groups. Such occasional statements can usually be traced to a period in history when Jews were physically tortured and religiously persecuted by their neighbours. In order to buoy the spirits of the downtrodden Jews, to give them hope that the end had not come, the ultimate downfall of other groups (i.e., the enemy) was predicted and the final vindication of Judaism as the One True religion was propounded.

Research in Jewish studies has pointed out the historic circumstances which gave rise to such attitudes. In our own day, various Jewish groups are working on their own, as well as in co-operation with Protestant and Catholic scholars, to correct and change the references to contemporary religious groups in unfriendly terms.

Part of the maturing relationship between diverse religious groups involves the acceptance of the lapses within a tradition from the best in itself. The "hate-monger" generalizes about a total group and its outlook from isolated expressions of negative statements of one group about another. The reflective seeker after truth understands the historic and psychological considerations which can, at times, cause one group to criticize or even vilify another and to elevate its own beliefs over those of its neighbours. There are poetic references in Jewish tradition to indicate that even angels argue and compete. All the more must one expect this from finite man. It is encouraging to note, however, that angels cannot improve; man can!

It must again be underscored that activities which advance respect for diversity of religious expression are not based on considerations of expediency and the desire to be "co-operative" (not that such motivation is in itself unpraiseworthy), but on the Jewish conviction that it is God's will that the diverse religious groups live together in mutual respect and peace. Only with such co-operation and understanding can the truths of His Kingdom be advanced, enabling man to resist the many expressions of idolatry and paganism current today. This view has been propounded with great poignancy by Doctor Louis Finkelstein.

The need for Universal Brotherhood among men is no longer merely a pious aspiration; it is the most urgent of all practical human needs. Until we can achieve it, we shall have to look forward for endless generations to the heavy burden of armament, living under constant threat of war and the continual peril to our country and to all civilized values.

The need to live together in mutual respect has today reached global proportions. Universal Brotherhood has to be made part of the daily thinking of each one of us, and we have all to re-dedicate ourselves regularly to this ancient Prophetic and Rabbinic concept. . . .

The concepts of the brotherhood of man as the child and creature of God, and of truth as a mode of communion with God, are common to all Western religions, which are based on the Scriptures. There is thus a vast field open for cooperation between the faiths in the advancement of these beliefs. This is not to imply that any energies needed to preserve the distinctive faith should be diverted from that purpose. There can be no religion in the modern world unless there are traditional religions. Judaism and the various forms of Christianity have each in their distinctive ways an enormous contribution to make to the preservation and furtherance of civilized life. But beyond the service which each can render separately, there are the goals toward which they must strive in common and, so far as America is concerned, can only attain in common. . . .

One sentence in this statement requires special emphasis in any programme for "good will" and co-operation between religious groups: "This is not to imply that any energies needed to preserve the distinctive faiths should be diverted from that purpose."

Genuine respect—and not simply tolerance—of other ways which lead to God does not mean that we seek a syncretistic, over-all religion which becomes all things to all people. Acceptance of the reality of diversity does not mean the weakening of one's deep commitment to the uniqueness and special quality of one's faith and its particularities. The challenge is to deepen the roots of one's faith in the soil of one's historic religious tradition, while recognizing that other religions are simultaneously planting and nurturing the gardens of their own historic faith with love, intensity, and integrity.

We have seen then that acceptance of diversity within the unity of mankind under one God is one of the pillars on which the Jewish view of inter-group relations rests. The second, and equally vital pillar of the structure, may be summarized as follows: Man, in the limited, finite conditions of his existence finds himself living this paradox: his own tradition is sacred, unique, and precious to him but, at the same time, he recognizes the right, the need, and the fact that others feel the same way about their own, differing historic traditions. This second principle might therefore be called the right to a feeling of uniqueness.

Within the framework of Judaism, the only limitation to this acceptance of differences is the basic core of moral principles—the Noachide Laws described above—which are regarded as binding on all men. Respect and tolerance stop at the door of the criminal, the tyrant, the beast—for individuals as well as for groups.

In a world which is fast becoming one large neighbourhood, understanding between religions of the East and West is as crucial as the relation between Protestant, Catholic, and Jew. What is more, diverse economic systems and cultural patterns are as much a part of the world neighbourhood as the variety of religious outlooks. In these areas, too, the principles of diversity within unity and the right to a feeling of uniqueness are vital for the survival of a complex civilization. Little wonder, then, that these requisites for peace, even in areas other than the specifically religious, have their roots in the Biblical view of the world.

This Biblical view of man's right to and need for a sense of unique purpose helps clarify an aspect of the Jewish attitude towards inter-group relations which is frequently confusing, if not misleading. Judaism has been pictured as accepting the diverse religious groups as authoritative and sacred for their respective constituents. How is this view reconciled with the references in its literature to the Jews as a "chosen people"? On the face of it, a "chosen people" suggests a superiority and arrogance which seem of a very different texture than the pattern that has been woven earlier. Here again, various sources help to demonstrate that what is now said is not an adjustment of Jewish thought to twentieth-century conditions, but rather reflects the authentic commitment of the tradition.

A fifth-century text reads as follows:

"And ye shall be holy unto Me, for I the Lord am holy and have set you apart from the people." (Lev. 20:26) Had the verse been written, "I have set people apart from you," then no other nation would have a chance of existing. However, the verse says: "I set you apart from Peoples" as one separates the good from the bad and then *returns* and separates the good from the bad again [Pesikta].

According to this teaching, the Almighty *chose* the Jews at a period in history for a specific function. This does not exclude the possibility of other peoples being chosen for other purposes. On this issue, Maimonides says:

> But it is beyond the human mind to fathom the designs of the Creator; for our ways are not His ways, neither are our thoughts His thoughts. All these matters relating to Jesus of Nazareth and the Ishmaelite [Mohammed] who came after him, only served to clear the way for King Messiah, to prepare the world to worship God....

In the passage from Martin Buber quoted earlier, the psychological, indeed theological, need of each man and group to have a sense of being *chosen, unique,* is stressed. "He is unique in the world in his particular character and that there has never been anyone like him in the world, for if there had been someone like him, there would have been no need for him to be in the world." Much of modern man's frustration and unhappiness derive from the technological and ideological conformity which levels all people to drab, tedious carbon copies of one another. A sense of individual and group goal in life is missing. To have such a sense of purpose is to feel *chosen*. It does not mean that others—individuals and groups —cannot have a sense of being *chosen*, too.

Perhaps this can be clarified further by comparing the feelings involved in another area of human experience. Jewish tradition prescribes that the father of the household recite chapter 31 of Proverbs upon returning home from the synagogue on Friday night. Verse twenty-nine reads as follows: "Many daughters have done valiantly *but thou excelleth them all*." The man reciting this verse is, in effect, saying: "My wife is the *best in the world*; she is *chosen*." Indeed, he must know upon the slightest reflection that many men, observing the same commandment, are expressing the same thought about their wives. Yet between husband and wife, deep love and a unique relationship are possible only if there are moments when they genuinely feel that they were chosen for one another. Again, this does not mean that one denies the right of other couples to feel the same way. However, the worst way to express commitment and love to a wife (or a husband) is in the words of the careful, logical, "honest" lover who at the height of his feeling declares: "You are the best wife, of course, *for me.*"

As with a mate, so too in relation to one's tradition and God one must experience moments of a unique, *chosen* relationship. In what Martin Buber calls the "I–Thou" relationship of man's confrontation with his Maker, there must be depths of feeling that know no qualification. Each of the diverse religious groups has this right to feel so keenly about its tradition. Mature relationships between diverse groups accept the paradoxical circumstances of such feeling as part of the complexity of man's finite existence.

The Talmud, the comprehensive source of Rabbinic law and lore, insists that practice is more important than theory. The Jewish community in North America adheres to this teaching in the area of inter-group relations. Each of the three major groups—Orthodox, Conservative, and Reform—are organized into lay bodies as well as associations of Rabbis. They all have committees on social action which address themselves to everyday issues of human rights and brotherhood. The following statement of the Central Conference of American Rabbis exemplifies the attitude of all three:

> The extent of a nation's respect for the dignity and rights of all its citizens is the full measure of its contribution to human progress. This concern for the dignity and rights of our citizens is embodied in the Bill of Rights which in turn finds divine sanction in the prophetic mandate, "Justice, Justice shalt thou pursue."

Even more compelling evidence for the present involvement of the Jewish community in the area of social justice and the advancement of inter-group understanding is the activities of the major seminaries on the American scene. A seminary is a training school for Rabbis. Orthodox Jews look to the Yeshiva University in New York as the fountainhead of their movement. In addition to the training of Rabbis, Yeshiva University recently organized a School of Education which gives advanced courses for public school teachers regardless of race or religion. The curriculum addresses itself to problems which are of concern to Americans of all races and religions. Similarly, the Reform Rabbinical Seminary, the Hebrew Union College in Cincinnati, conducts institutes on Judaism for Christian ministers. The underlying assumption of the programme is that advancing understanding and respect between the Jewish and Christian communities—genuine brotherhood—is the responsibility of a Jewish seminary. Finally, Conservative Jews draw their leadership and guidance from the Jewish Theological Seminary of America in New York. The purpose of the Institute of the Religious and Social Studies of this Seminary is described in its register as "to develop a keener awareness of the unique contributions which the various religious traditions have made to the advancement of civilization; and can make toward solution of the perplexities of our day." The publications of this Institute comprise the largest collection of studies from any one source on inter-group relations in America.

When seminaries, organized for the training of Rabbis and sectarian religious teachers, see the advancement of brotherhood as part of their vital concern, the atmosphere of love of neighbour, respect for differences, trust, and genuine fellowship can permeate the entire community. The peace which can result from the intensification of such efforts is indispensable, not alone for human advancement, but for the very survival of our society.

12 / Ethical Considerations in the Shaping of Jewish Life

SIMON GREENBERG

Any thoughtful individual who is engaged in activities that of necessity leave their impress upon Jewish life in his community cannot but be challenged from time to time by the question "What ethical considerations should guide us as we strive to shape Jewish life?" From time to time we all feel the need to find answers to this question and hunger for an opportunity to discuss it with colleagues. Yet we rarely do so, except for a brief moment now and then.

We avoid discussing fundamentals for many reasons. We are part of a society that is not philosophically minded, which values action above all and suspects that abstract thought of any kind is an impediment to action. Moreover, human experience offers innumerable examples of men co-operating in the achievement of a common task, without agreeing upon the "considerations" which move each one of them to want the task accomplished. Discussion of fundamental principles, of underlying considerations, ethical or otherwise, which give philosophic breadth and depth to an enterprise are therefore considered to be not only the wasteful diversion of time and energy, but also dangerous to its success. Such discussion may reveal differences that might lead to tensions and misunderstandings among the working partners.

There is much truth to this pragmatic approach to the problems of human co-operative effort. It is easy enough, for example, to get everyone to agree that a hospital is a most useful and worthy institution. But if the building of a hospital by a Jewish community were to depend upon reaching agreement regarding the considerations—ethical or otherwise—which should motivate the effort, the chances are that interminable debate would lead to a stalemate, even in this area comparatively so amenable to theoretic agreement.

We all are fully conscious of the weaknesses inherent in the purely pragmatic approach. Though man is not an exclusively rational animal, rationality is nevertheless a very significant factor in the totality of his endowments. His reason incessantly presses its demands upon him, and these cannot be ignored indefinitely with impunity. Reason, by the very nature of its being, insists upon relating acts to several principles, concepts, or considerations. When individuals co-operating in a common task relate it rationally to different basic concepts or principles, the co-operative effort is sooner or later subjected to severe strain. For sooner or later each one of the co-operating groups seeks to fashion the institution more nearly in the image of its own basic motivating concept or consideration. The suppressed tension eventually comes to the fore. Even when it does not completely disrupt the co-operating group, it often generates subconscious discontent within groups, discontent that saps the group's spiritual and emotional vitality and is ultimately reflected in the slackening of physical effort and the desultory character of the group's activities. In the long run, therefore, the widest possible agreement on general considerations is indispensable to effective, purposeful group action.

A community whose life is shaped merely by pragmatic reactions to the immediate problems it may face, day-to-day, may at the moment appear to be vigorous and even successful. But a community, even more than an individual, must be aware of some purpose or purposes to which its acts as a community are consciously and rationally related. Without such awareness of the integrating principles of its being, it is bound to disintegrate.

The theme before us in this paper calls for a discussion of the *ethical* considerations that shape Jewish life. A discussion of what it is that makes a "consideration" ethical would probably be interesting and enjoyable. I must assume, however, that there is adequate general agreement on the meaning of the term *"ethical* considerations," and proceed to name what I believe to be the "considerations" that *are* shaping or *should* shape Jewish life. I shall name them not in what in my opinion is the order of their merit, but in the order of their current pervasiveness. They are: the need for personal status; self-defence; Jewish survival; the sense of mutual dependence and of obligation towards the less favourably situated; the search for meaning and purpose in human life; *Talmud Torah* —as Jewish self-knowledge and as life-long intellectual and spiritual growth rooted in the study of the Bible, Rabbinic literature and of Jewish history, thought and literature; Judaism as an all-embracing pattern and philosophy of life; and, finally, *Kiddush Hashem*, the sanctification and glorification of God's name in one's personal life as well as in the life of the community. This list of considerations will appear too long to some and too short to others, but even if the list needs correction, it is adequate for the purpose that I have in mind. In relation to it I propose to ask a number of questions.

How many people active in shaping Jewish life today ever take the trouble to relate their activities to more than one or two of the considerations herein listed? How many Jewish leaders ask themselves whether what they are doing and asking others to do is related not only to self-defence or status, but also to *Talmud Torah*, or *Kiddush Hashem*, or purpose and meaning in life? How many Jewish leaders concerned primarily with *Talmud Torah* or with the search for meaning in life, take the trouble to relate their particular consideration to all the others? Limited concern mars the ethical essence of any activity, regardless of how ethical the consideration to which it is specifically related may in itself be. I do not decry activities motivated by considerations of self-defence. Certainly I do not belittle activities related to *Talmud Torah*. But when any one of these considerations is viewed by its devotees and urged upon others as the all-sufficient, all-inclusive consideration for the shaping of Jewish life, a quality is ascribed to it which it does not possess. It is burdened with a task that it is incapable of performing and the unbearable weight warps and deforms its character and quality. Hence, my first suggestion—and perhaps the most important—is that at the top of the list of ethical considerations that should shape Jewish life we should place this question: How is the specific activity in which you are engaged related to all or at least most of the ethical considerations herein listed?

Our most flagrant and most dangerous ethical shortcoming has been over-specialization. Our leaders have by and large not been *Jewish* leaders but *Zionist* leaders, *B'nai Brith* leaders, *Synagogue* leaders, *Federation* leaders, and so forth. Now, specialization has unquestionably been one of the secrets of the success of the modern world in science, business, and scholarship. But it is also in very large measure responsible for the fact that in an age in which means of communication have unimaginable range and efficiency, mankind is divided into a greater number of hostile groups than ever before, and in an age in which more and more people master smaller and smaller areas of skill and knowledge, an ever decreasing number of people possess that scope of comprehension, that universality of sentiment, that breadth and depth of understanding of life which are the unmistakable characteristics of the truly civilized, as opposed to the merely trained, human being.

Because of this high degree of specialization, individual Jewish leaders, and the organizations they head, have attained unprecedented success. We have never had as many successful drives and organizations and there is probably no other group in America which has so large a proportion of its members affiliated with and contributing to, some good cause. None the less, anyone who is close to Jewish life cannot but feel that we have not as yet succeeded in creating an over-all image of ourselves beyond that of being the group that has developed the most aggressive fund-raising techniques in the world. Do not misunderstand me: I have a great and sincere respect for those who developed such techniques. They have performed a most necessary service for a group which cannot exercise the power of compulsory taxation, and performed it during a period when our people were facing unprecedented crises. But we would not serve our people properly if we were to close our eyes to the fact that in times of crises things are done and techniques are employed which in more normal times cannot and should not be allowed.

For example, there can be no doubt that no consideration is more powerful than that of self-defence in calling forth an immediate and desired response. Nor is there any doubt that the drive for status is second only to self-defence as a motive for acts of generosity and of courage verging on the heroic. But these two drives are intrinsically not ethical considerations. There is nothing intrinsically ethical in wanting to defend oneself either as an individual or as a group, and there is certainly nothing intrinsically ethical in seeking for oneself or for one's group a position of power, or of regard in relation to others. The ethical qualities of these two considerations depend therefore exclusively on the quality of the means that are employed to achieve them. At the same time, no other considerations, no other ends sanctify more means, in the eyes of more people, than do self-defence and status.

Another ethical danger, inherent in both these otherwise very legitimate ends, is a sense of their all-sufficiency. One is easily convinced that he has fulfilled his duty as a Jew if he has made some contribution towards Jewish self-defence or towards attaining what he would consider satisfactory status for the Jew. Let me repeat that I do not believe that there is anything inherently wrong with either activity. On the contrary, I consider both not only legitimate but indispensable. I do believe, however, that these take on unethical qualities more easily than the others I have noted, because they lend themselves most readily to the ethical perversion of means, and to the sense of their being all-sufficient.

What I have said about self-defence and status applies only a little less strongly to most of the other considerations I have listed. Most of them are subject to the corruptions of being used as justification for unethical means or of being expounded as all-sufficient for the shaping of Jewish life.

You will note that I have not listed "Jewish unity or solidarity" as an ethical consideration in its own right. Its inclusion in the list can be readily justified. Yet I have not included it because I do not consider unity *per se*, any more than "sincerity" *per se*, an ethical consideration. Unity and sincerity derive their ethical quality from the cause or object regarding which a group is united or an individual is sincere.

It has long been my conviction that our protestations regarding the virtues of Jewish unity founder on the rocks of institutional loyalites as well as of philosophic parochialism. Too often we invoke "unity" only because we want the institution with which we are associated to flourish, too often our philosophy of Jewish life makes no room for what the other fellow is doing. Thus it is not sufficient for us to say that we admit the right of those who think that *Talmud Torah* is important to pursue activities that encourage it. We must, if we want to arrive at true and meaningful Jewish unity, find room for *Talmud Torah* in our own thinking and incorporate it in some measure in the activity that is of immediate concern to us. Jewish unity achieved primarily on the institutional level—a goal which at the moment appears to be wholly beyond probability (for the Jews of the United States at any rate)—may have the virtue of exposing all of us to one another's convictions and beliefs and thus eventually broadening everyone's horizons. But it may also prove to be a spiritual and intellectual catastrophe, for it may result in a unity based upon the lowest common denominator. A Jewish community united organizationally can be a spiritual blessing to us only if the programme of activities of such a community is consciously and effectively related to all of the considerations I have listed.

On the other hand, institutionally disparate activities which are rooted in the totality of the considerations listed, will bestow upon Jewish life a unity which is far more significant than the unity achieved through an organizational structure based upon only one or two of these considerations. Jewish history knows only very few short-lived periods of institutionalized unity, such as the era of David and Solomon and, to a lesser degree, the Hasmonean period. During the long periods of exile and dispersion the exemplary unity we did manage to maintain was rooted in the fact that disjointed Jewish communities and organizations were rooted in a large number of shared ethical considerations.

The second question I propose to ask in relation to my list of ethical considerations is this: Are they all of equal ethical significance? If they are not, and I believe we could readily agree that they are not, then it becomes proper and necessary to try to arrange them not in the order of present pervasiveness (as I have), but rather in the order of their ethical significance. If we were to do so we would soon discover that the order of my list must be completely reversed. In my opinion, we would all agree that the consideration which ought to be the most pervasive in shaping Jewish life is the one which our tradition has designated as *Kiddush Hashem*—the sanctification of God's name in one's personal life and in the life of the community. I believe it is high time that this noblest of all ethical concepts of our tradition should be re-introduced into the daily speech of our people for there is no other concept which expresses so effectively the ultimate goal of all of Jewish life. To sanctify God's name is to live in accordance with the injunctions of the nineteenth chapter of Leviticus. It is to love one's neighbour as oneself, to love the stranger, to bear no grudge, to deal honestly and fairly, not to curse the deaf or put a stumbling block before the blind. It is to do all this not because it will make you acceptable in the eyes of your neighbour, nor because it will bring you worldly success, but because this is how one expresses one's love for God and fulfils oneself as a creature made in the image of God.

The responsibility for re-introducing this ethical consideration into the life of the Jewish community rests primarily but not exclusively upon the shoulders of the Rabbinate. All those to whom the Jewish community looks for guidance must ever be conscious of the primary role that *Kiddush Hashem* should play in shaping Jewish life. For, of the considerations I have listed, *Kiddush Hashem* is the only one which is intrinsically ethical, which is simultaneously means and end, and which alone is the indispensable ingredient in all the other considerations if they are justifiably to be described as ethical. The great tragedy of Jewish life is that in our zeal to defend ourselves and to win status, and even to teach *Torah*, we forget that without *Kiddush Hashem*, without personal integrity and clean hands, none of these considerations have any particular ethical significance.

If it is Jewish life that we are interested in shaping, what is there which makes life "Jewish" even in the State of Israel in a more significant and positive manner than *Talmud Torah?* Eliminate *Talmud Torah* from the activities of the Jewish community and you are left with Jews but not with Jewish life. There are some encouraging signs of late that the role of *Talmud Torah* in shaping Jewish life is expanding. But it is as yet very far from being as pervasive and effective a factor in our lives as are self-defence or status-seeking.

It is impossible to discuss even briefly all of the considerations I have listed. I cannot, however, conclude this paper without commenting briefly on the role of the State of Israel in shaping Jewish life in America. As a lifelong Zionist who believes that an independent, economically and physically secure, spiritually sensitive, politically democratic State of Israel is indispensable to the welfare of the Jewish people and the full flowering of Judaism everywhere, it was but natural for me to include in my first list of considerations, "support of the State of Israel." But upon further reflection it became increasingly clear to me that support of the State of Israel is subsumed in one aspect or another under almost every one of the other considerations listed: defence, status, Jewish survival, sense of obligation to the less-privileged, and so on. But very few among us support the State of Israel, *per se*. On the contrary, American Jews, as Jews everywhere outside the State of Israel, repeatedly and rightfully declare that they neither owe nor feel any attachment to the State as a political entity but only to those aspects of its activities which relate it to the considerations I have listed, and only to the extent that it is thus related. The basic problem of the future relationship between the State of Israel and world Jewry generally is how to relate the State significantly to the considerations I have listed so that concern for its welfare may remain a vital force shaping Jewish life everywhere.

Finally, as one whose life has been moulded from the very beginning by the Synagogue, not as a House of Study or of Meeting, but primarily as a House of Prayer, you will, I hope, not accuse me of making a plea *pro domo* when I say that with all of its shortcomings—and no one is more aware of these than I—the Synagogue remains the one institution in Jewish life which brings the message of other institutions to its members. No hospital board discusses Jewish educational problems, no Zionist district talks about the health needs of the community. Agencies for defence do not consider it their duty to urge their members to build Synagogues. It is only from the pulpit of the Synagogue that the totality of the considerations that should mould Jewish life is embraced. Indeed the weakness of the Synagogue as a national organization is in large measure due to its being on the local level the most comprehensive of all institutions in its programme and concerns.

It is the expansion of the horizons of the leaders of all the institutions that shape Jewish life which I believe to be a prime prerequisite of our day. Simultaneously with this must come the realization that, in the shaping of Jewish life, centrality must be given to the concept of *Kiddush Hashem*, the sanctification and glorification of God's name.

Contributors

Contributors

JOHN C. BENNETT, A.B., William College; A.B., Oxford University; M.A., B.D., S.T.M., Union Theological Seminary; honorary doctorates, Church Divinity School of the Pacific, Pacific School of Religion, William College. Author, *Social Salvations; Christianity and our World; Christian Realism, Christian Ethics and Social Policy; Christianity and Communism; Christianity and Communism Today; The Christian as Citizen; Christian Values and Economic Life;* co-author, *Christians and the State.* Dean of the Faculty, Union Theological Seminary, New York.

Lecture delivered at Beth Tzedec Congregation, May 10, 1961.

BROCK CHISHOLM, C.B.E., M.D., University of Toronto; honorary degrees, University of North Carolina, University of British Columbia; Brandeis University; PH.D., University of Nancy (France). Author, *William Alanson White Memorial Lectures; Prescription for Survival; Can People Learn to Learn.* Formerly Director-General, World Health Organization, United Nations.

Lecture delivered at Beth Tzedec Congregation, March 15, 1961.

PAUL H. DOUGLAS, B.A., Bowdoin College; PH.D., Columbia University. Author, *American Apprenticeship and Industrial*

166 / CONTRIBUTORS

Education; The Worker in Modern Economic Society; Wages and the Family; Adam Smith; Real Wages in the United States; The Coming of a New Party; Standards of Unemployment Insurance; Theory of Wages; Controlling Depressions; Ethics in Government; Economy in the National Government. United States Senator from Illinois.

Lecture delivered at Beth Tzedec Congregation, February 22, 1961.

THOMAS M. EBERLEE, B.A., University of Toronto. Assistant Secretary of Provincial Cabinet (Ontario); Secretary, Human Rights Commission (Ontario); Secretary, Goldenberg Commission on Labour Management Relation in Construction Industry.

Lecture delivered at Beth Tzedec Congregation, March 29, 1961.

LOUIS FINE, civil servant, Provincial Government; Chief Conciliation Officer, Province of Ontario; Director, Fair Employment Practices; Chairman, Human Rights Commission, Province of Ontario.

Lecture delivered at Beth Tzedec Congregation, March 29, 1961.

LOUIS FINKELSTEIN, A.B., College of City of New York; PH.D., Columbia University; Rabbi, Jewish Theological Seminary of America; (Hon.) S.T.D., Columbia University; (Hon.) D.L., Boston University. Author, *Jewish Self-Government in the Middle Ages; The Pharisees; Prolegomena to an Edition of the Sifre; The Mekilta and its Texts; Akiba—Scholar, Saint, Martyr; Belief and Practices of Judaism; The Jews: Their History, Culture and Religion* (ed.). Chancellor and President of the Faculties, Jewish Theological Seminary of America, New York.

SIMON GREENBERG, B.A., College of the City of New York; Rabbi, Jewish Theological Seminary of America; PH.D., Dropsie College. Author, *Living as a Jew Today; Ideals and Values of the Jewish Prayer Book; the First Year in the Hebrew School, A Teacher's Guide.* Vice-Chancellor, Jewish Theological Seminary of America, New York.

Lecture delivered at Beth Tzedec Congregation, April 27, 1961.

Contributors / 167

MORDECAI W. JOHNSON, A.B., Morehouse College; B.D., Rochester Theological Seminary; S.T.M., Harvard University; honorary degrees, Howard University, Morehouse College, Gammon Theological Seminary, Delaware State College, University of Liberia, Virginia State College; honorary doctorates, Colby College, Temple University, Michigan State College, University of Liberia, Virginia State College. President Emeritus, Howard University.

Lecture delivered at Beth Tzedec Congregation, March 29, 1961.

BERNARD MANDELBAUM, B.A., Columbia University; Rabbi, M.H.L., D.H.L., Jewish Theological Seminary of America. Editor, *Assignment in Israel*. Provost, Jewish Theological Seminary of America, New York.

Lecture delivered at Beth Tzedec Congregation, May 10, 1961.

STUART E. ROSENBERG, B.A., Brooklyn College; Rabbi, M.H.L., Jewish Theological Seminary of America; M.A., PH.D., Columbia University. Author, *The Bible is for You*; *Bridge to Brotherhood*; *A Time to Speak*; *The Road to Confidence*; *Man is Free*; *The Jewish Community in Rochester*. Rabbi, Beth Tzedec Congregation, Toronto, Canada.

MURRAY G. ROSS, B.A., Acadia University; M.A., University of Toronto; ED.D., Columbia University. Author, *The New University*; *Case Histories in Community Organization*; *New Understandings of Leadership*; *Community Organization: Theory and Principles*; *The Y.M.C.A. in Canada*; *Religious Beliefs of Youth*; *Towards Professional Maturity* (ed.). President, York University, Toronto, Ontario.

Lecture delivered at Beth Tzedec Congregation, April 12, 1961.

ANDREW STEWART, B.S.A., East of Scotland Agricultural College, Edinburgh; M.A., University of Manitoba, Winnipeg; LL.D., Manitoba, New Brunswick, Melbourne, Alberta; D.SC.ECON., Laval University. Fellow, Agricultural Institute of Canada, Royal Society of Canada. Chairman, Board of Broadcast Governors, Government of Canada.

Lecture delivered at Beth Tzedec Congregation, February 8, 1961.

www.ingramcontent.com/pod-product-compliance
Lightning Source LLC
Chambersburg PA
CBHW020413080526
44584CB00014B/1315